22/4/93 (AS)
BUCKS HQ
10/3/98
14 JUN 2002
2 8 JAN 2004
2 3 JUL 2012

0 8 JAN 2013

This book is to be returned on or before the date above.
It may be borrowed for a further period if not in demand.

HW   75413   LIBRARIES

WRITER-FILES

General Editor: Simon Trussler

Associate Editor: Malcolm Page

File on FUGARD

Compiled by Stephen Gray

Methuen Drama

A Methuen Drama Book
First published in 1991 as a paperback original
by Methuen Drama, Michelin House,
81 Fulham Road, London SW3 6RB,
and distributed in the USA by
HEB Inc., 361 Hanover Street, Portsmouth,
New Hampshire, NH 03801 3959

Copyright in the compilation
© 1991 by Stephen Gray
Copyright in the series format
© 1991 by Methuen Drama
Copyright in the editorial presentation
© 1991 by Simon Trussler
The author has asserted his moral rights

Typeset in 9/10 Times by
L. Anderson Typesetting,
Woodchurch, Kent TN26 3TB

Printed in Great Britain
by Cox and Wyman Ltd.,
Cardiff Road, Reading

ISBN 413 64580 0

British Library Cataloguing in Publication Data
is available from the British Library

Picture of Fugard reproduced
by kind permission of Mary Benson

This paperback edition is sold subject to the
condition that it shall not, by way of trade or
otherwise, be lent, resold, hired out, or otherwise
circulated without the publisher's prior consent in
any form of binding or cover other than that in
which it is published and without a similar condition
including this condition being imposed on the
subsequent purchaser

Contents

General Editor's Introduction	5
1: A Brief Chronology	7
2: The Plays	11
a: Stage Plays	
Klaas and the Devil	11
The Cell	11
No-Good Friday	11
Nongogo	14
The Blood Knot	16
Hello and Goodbye	25
The Coat	30
People Are Living There	31
The Last Bus	35
Boesman and Lena	35
Friday's Bread on Monday	39
Orestes	40
Statements after an Arrest under the Immorality Act	43
Sizwe Bansi Is Dead	45
The Island	49
Dimetos	52
A Lesson from Aloes	54
The Drummer	57
'Master Harold' . . . and the Boys	57
The Road to Mecca	61
A Place with the Pigs	64
My Children! My Africa!	67
b: Television Plays	
The Occupation	70
Mille Miglia	70
c: Feature Films	
Boesman and Lena	71
The Guest	72
Marigolds in August	73
3: Non-Dramatic Writing	
a: Novel	75
b: Autobiography	76
4: The Writer on His Work	77
5: A Select Bibliography	85

General Editor's Introduction

The theatre is, by its nature, an ephemeral art: yet it is a daunting task to track down the newspaper reviews, or contemporary statements from the writer or his director, which are often all that remain to help us recreate some sense of what a particular production was like. This series is therefore intended to make readily available a selection of the comments that the critics made about the plays of leading modern dramatists at the time of their production — and to trace, too, the course of each writer's own views about his work and his world.

In addition to combining a uniquely convenient source of such elusive *documentation*, the 'Writer-Files' series also assembles the *information* necessary for readers to pursue further their interest in a particular writer or work. Variations in quantity between one writer's output and another's, differences in temperament which make some readier than others to talk about their work, and the variety of critical response, all mean that the presentation and balance of material shifts between one volume and another: but we have tried to arrive at a format for the series which will nevertheless enable users of one volume readily to find their way around any other.

Section 1, 'A Brief Chronology', provides a quick conspective overview of each playwright's life and career. *Section 2* deals with the plays themselves, arranged chronologically in the order of their composition: information on first performances, major revivals, and publication is followed by a brief synopsis (for quick reference set in slightly larger, italic type), then by a representative selection of the critical response, and of the dramatist's own comments on the play and its theme.

Section 3 offers concise guidance to each writer's work in non-dramatic forms, while *Section 4*, 'The Writer on His Work', brings together comments from the playwright himself on more general matters of construction, opinion, and artistic development. Finally, *Section 5* provides a bibliographical guide to other primary and secondary sources of further reading, among which full details will be found of works cited elsewhere under short titles, and of collected editions of the plays — but not of individual titles, particulars of which will be found with the other factual data in Section 2.

The 'Writer-Files' hope by striking this kind of balance between information and a wide range of opinion to offer 'companions' to the study of major playwrights in the modern repertoire — not in that dangerous pre-digested fashion which

5

General Editor's Introduction

can too readily quench the desire to read the plays themselves, nor so prescriptively as to allow any single line of approach to predominate, but rather to encourage readers to form their own judgements of the plays in a wide-ranging context.

Athol Fugard is a 'classic example of the guilt-ridden, impotent white liberal of South Africa' — that, at least, is his own wry verdict, recorded on page 81 of this 'Writer-File'. And perhaps the urgent drive of that guilt and the underlying energy of impotence together give his plays a double cutting-edge which, in any other culture, they might have lacked. Certainly, the multiplicity of comparisons with other writers made by the critics represented in this volume — with Brecht, Beckett, Pinter, Mercer, even the old-style naturalists — is seldom to his disadvantage, because any occasional resemblances of mood or style are, as Stanley Kauffmann puts it on page 38, 'rooted in such a felt need': the need of the dramatist to respond with conviction and with craftsmanship to the tragic circumstances of his historic place and time.

The South African critic Ian Steadman makes a distinction on pages 68-9 between plays which show 'how people should cope with things as they are' and those which reveal 'how things can and should be changed'. Fugard has written plays of both kinds and neither, but the centre of gravity has tended to shift from the former, 'domesticating' variety to the latter, 'liberating' mode — as *The Blood Knot* and *My Children! My Africa!* at each end of his career to date suggest. However, as he discussed at some length in a lecture given in 1990, reprinted here on pages 83-4, Fugard will now need to accommodate the new hopes for his country, whether these are to be fulfilled or dashed — as a South African, of course, but also as a *playwright*, who stresses his pride, as he might in being a wheelwright or a shipwright, in the down-to-earth nature of his chosen trade.

We are thus reminded in this volume (not least by the factual data) of the range and depth of Fugard's acting and directing experience, as of those occasional forays into 'collective creation' which have nourished his more orthodox writing. The compiler has, valuably, included a range not only of South African opinions, both black and white, but also of reactions to the plays worldwide: for, however culturally-specific their content appears, they *work*, it seems, everywhere they have been staged. They are intensely (not least linguistically) pin-downable, often speaking of infinite poverty in a little room, yet their very specificity has paradoxically widened their appeal. No more than a revolution superseded Chekhov, or improvements in Norwegian sanitation made Ibsen's *An Enemy of the People* redundant, need we worry that the hopefully imminent ending of apartheid will 'date' the plays of Athol Fugard.

Simon Trussler

1: A Brief Chronology

1932 11 June, Harold Athol Lannigan Fugard born in the town of Middelburg, Cape Province, in the heart of the South African Great Karoo semi-desert, where his parents own a general cash store. His mother (née Potgieter) is Afrikaans-speaking and his father Anglo-Irish; he remains fluently bilingual, but the family's home language is English.

1935 The family, which includes a brother and sister, moves to the coastal city of Port Elizabeth, Eastern Province, where he will always be based.

1938-49 Schooling in Port Elizabeth. From 1941 Mrs. Fugard takes over the Saint George's Park Tea Room near the swimming baths, as depicted in *'Master Harold' ... and the Boys*. Hard times for the family, owing partly to the crippled father's invalidism (used in *Hello and Goodbye*).

1950-52 Scholarship to the University of Cape Town to study philosophy.

1953-54 Drops out to hitch-hike up Africa to the Sudan, and to work his passage around the world on a tramp-steamer. Frequently comments that he was fortunate to have experienced Africa before Europe and been cured of 'colour prejudice' early on. Writes first articles about his voyages, short stories, and poems.

1955-57 Regional news reporter, transferred from Port Elizabeth to Cape Town. Marries Sheila Meiring, actress; they form a theatre workshop performing his one-acters in the style of Synge and O'Neill, directed by her.

1958 Clerk in the Fordsburg Native Commissioner's Court, Johannesburg — 'the ugliest thing I've every been part of' ('Afrikaner Humanist', *The Observer*, 18 July 1971). While the Treason Trial continues, *No-Good Friday* premiered for the African Theatre Workshop. Fugard is employed as a stage-manager by the National Theatre organization.

1959 *Nongogo* premiered in Johannesburg.

1960 London; scripts turned down by the Royal Court. Fugard and Sheila join the New Africa Group in the Low Countries and Fugard acts in the prize-winning entry at the

A Brief Chronology

Festival of Avant-Garde Theatre, Brussels. 21 March, Sharpeville massacre and five-month state of emergency in South Africa. They return home, he working on his novel *Tsotsi*, *The Blood Knot*, and his notebooks — published entries date from here.

1961 27 May, daughter Lisa born and *The Blood Knot* completed. 31 May, South Africa becomes a republic, expelled from the British Commonwealth, and the 'apartheid' system becomes entrenched. September, *The Blood Knot* premiered, and runs for four hours: cut version tours for six months.

1962 An open letter to British playwrights leads to their boycott of performances of their plays in segregated theatres. Works as a director for black theatre in the Rehearsal Room, Johannesburg.

1963 Begins his association with Serpent Players in Port Elizabeth, including directing adaptations of Machiavelli, Büchner, Soyinka, Camus, Brecht, Beckett, Genet, and Sophocles, the latter's *Antigone* as performed by Serpent Players becoming the core-play in *The Island*. Scripts devised with the Serpent Players include *The Coat* and *Sizwe Bansi Is Dead*. The action of *A Lesson from Aloes* is also set in these years of political clampdown and the going into imprisonment or exile of resisters. Purchases a house at Schoenmakerskop outside Port Elizabeth, which remains his home.

1965 *Hello and Goodbye* opens as the second of his 'Port Elizabethan' family plays.

1966 Briefly forms the Ijinle company to perform Soyinka and *The Blood Knot* at the Hampstead Theatre Club.

1967 Owing to the BBC-TV broadcast of *The Blood Knot*, Fugard's passport is withdrawn until the end of the decade.

1968 *People Are Living There* premiered in Glasgow without Fugard attending, and *Mille Miglia* televised.

1969 Fugard elected by *The Star* as man of the year in South Africa. *Boesman and Lena* premiered.

1971 The *Orestes* experiment leads to the founding of the (non-segregated) Space fringe theatre in Cape Town, which opens in 1972 with *Statements after an Arrest under the Immorality Act*, followed by *Sizwe Bansi Is Dead* and *The Island*. These transfer as a 'South African

A Brief Chronology

season' to the Royal Court, London, in 1973, and tour until 1974 including in the United States.

1972 Plays the lead in Mary Benson's radio adaptation of Sheila Fugard's novel, *The Castaways*, for the BBC. The BBC broadcasts and/or televises Fugard scripts from *The Blood Knot* through *Sizwe Bansi*, and most subsequent major works are filmed.

1974 Fugard reverses his opinion on the playwrights' boycott of South Africa and encourages dramatists to insist on performances in non-segregated venues. The Sheffield season of Fugard includes *The Blood Knot*, *No-Good Friday* and *Nongogo*.

1975 *Dimetos* commissioned for the Edinburgh Festival.

1976 16 June, the Soweto insurrection. 19 October, the Market Theatre opens in Johannesburg. With the decline of the Space this becomes Fugard's new artistic base.

1977 *The Guest* released.

1978 *A Lesson from Aloes* premiered at the Market.

1979 South African theatres desegregated, leading to a rich decade of indigenous playwriting and productions.

1980 Six months fellowship at Yale, which leads to a working relationship throughout the decade of try-outs in New Haven before Broadway premieres. He establishes a second home in Connecticut. *The Drummer* performed, and *Marigolds in August* released. His novel, *Tsotsi*, published after a twenty-year delay.

1981 *Aloes* exported from the Market to the National Theatre, London, beginning a working arrangement which includes the transfer of other Market productions to the UK (*'Master Harold' . . . and the Boys*, *The Road to Mecca*, *A Place with the Pigs* and *My Children! My Africa!*). Throughout the 'eighties, Fugard's own productions of his new plays are presented at Yale, the National, and the Market. He appears in Brook's *Meetings with Remarkable Men* (1979), Attenborough's *Gandhi* (1982), and *The Killing Fields* (1984).

1982 *'Master Harold' . . . and the Boys* premiered. In South Africa the script is banned, but the proscription set aside on appeal. BBC-2 shows a documentary, *Fugard's People*, by Helena Nogueira.

A Brief Chronology

1983 His *Notebooks (1960-77)* published, being the logbooks of his life and writing practice.

1984 While *The Guest* is showing on general release in New York, Fugard admits to having sworn off alcohol addiction. *The Road to Mecca* launched in the three countries (Broadway production delayed until 1988). This begins his collaboration with stage designer Douglas Heap, with Mannie Manim as lighting designer.

1986 Declaration of the second South African state of emergency.

1987 *A Place with the Pigs* premiered in the three countries.

1989 7 August, a *Time* magazine profile calls him 'the greatest active playwright in English'.

1990 Mandela released. *My Children! My Africa!* premiered in the three countries.

1991 August, new full-length play scheduled to open at the University of Witwatersrand Theatre, Johannesburg.

a: Stage Plays

Klaas and the Devil

Play in one act.
Written: for the Circle Players workshop, founded by him and
   Sheila Fugard, in Cape Town.
First production: Scopus Club, 3 Oct. 1956 (dir. Sheila
   Fugard).
Unpublished, and unavailable for production.

The Cell

Play in one act.
Written: for Circle Players.
First production: 1957.
Unpublished, and unavailable for production.

No-Good Friday

Full-length play in five scenes.
Written: in collaboration with the performers of the African
   Music and Drama Association, Dorkay House,
   Johannesburg.
First production: Bantu Men's Social Centre, Johannesburg,
   30 Aug. 1958 (dir. Fugard; with Stephen Moloi as Willie,
   Gladys Sibisi as Rebecca, Bloke Modisane as Shark, Ken
   Gampu as Tobias, Zakes Mokae as First Thug, and Fugard
   as Father Higgins).
First British production: Crucible Studio, Sheffield,
   6 Nov. 1974 (dir. Peter James; with Alton Kumalo as
   Willie, Merduee Jordine as Rebecca, and Jimi Rand as
   Guy).
Published: Dimetos and Two Early Plays (Oxford University
   Press, 1977).

The play is set in the 1950s in a backyard in the freehold township of Johannesburg's legendary

2: The Plays

No-Good Friday

Sophiatown (demolished in 1960), represented naturalistically with corrugated-iron walls and washing lines as a semi-public place. Within the set is Willie's study area. It is Friday night — traditionally pay-packet time when the streets are unsafe. Willie and Rebecca are at the end of a relationship which is being sacrificed to his aspirations as a student. Guy, a saxophone player in the township blues style of the time, is their best friend and go-between. The communal activity of the yard is threatened by a gang of cruising racketeers, headed by Shark. A 'blanket boy', Tobias, refuses to pay Shark protection money and, to the horror of the (white) priest, is murdered as a warning to other residents. In not confronting Shark on behalf of the residents of the yard, Willie loses Rebecca, and is then forced to choose between silence and promotion or taking action. He goes out to confront Shark.

Athol's first play dealing with the gang protection racket in Johannesburg townships was unashamedly sensational, but already in the powerful lyricism of some of its passages, its concern with the trapped individual, and the urgent need to resolve his problem by taking a stand, the work foreshadowed what was later to become the principal preoccupation of this playwright. The play, however, had very little concern with the politics behind the chronic violence and gangsterism in the ghetto. Consequently, it posed the wrong questions and provided the wrong answers.

Nevertheless, there was a certain quality in the writing which finally saved the play from degenerating altogether into a B-type gangster film of the Chicago genre. Fugard's manner of writing the play had been partly to make the actors improvise and then later to improve on their lines, or the other way around: to write the draft scenes and try them out with the actors, changing the material when necessary to fit a new situation. At the time we were all under the influence of the 'method' of Lee Strasberg's Actors Studio in New York. Bloke Modisane, for instance, was a great fan of Marlon Brando's and had listened countless times to Brando's Mark Antony speech. Since there is a great deal of 'ham' in the behaviour of Johannesburg thugs (after all, they too learn their parts from Hollywood films), Modisane's bravura and 'method' acting was no handicap. Indeed, he was splendid in the part.

Lewis Nkosi, 'Athol Fugard: His Work and Us',
South Africa: Information and Analysis,
Paris, No. 63 (May 1968), p. 3

No-Good Friday

During August [1958] Sheila and Athol Fugard came to see me [in Sophiatown] with a bottle of brandy and the request to fill a replacement in his new play, *No-Good Friday*; it was explained that there was no money in it, the actors pay their own expenses with only the promise that if it should make money the actor would share in the pool. The part was that of a gangster, Shark, a violent little man with an external charm and eruptions of violence which were locked inside the man.

We played before such small audiences it was discouraging, and it seemed that all the effort, the money, the sheer physical hard work Athol Fugard — without any backing, even from [AMDA], which only invested in certainties at the box-office — had put into it would have been in vain. The play was given two nights in a small hall in Johannesburg — the first before an all-white audience — and attracted the interest of a white impresario who booked the play for four nights in the white Brian Brooke Theatre; but this booking almost destroyed the play itself because Athol Fugard, the playwright and white man who plays the priest — a kind of Father Huddleston figure — was not allowed on the same stage with black actors, and Athol Fugard had accepted the principle without consulting the actors.

The actors confronted Athol with this betrayal, protesting that there was an agreement not to pander to the bigotry of white South Africa; the actors refused to perform without him in the cast, but he argued that it was a big break for the play, and we became sentimental and relented because it seemed to be his whole life, the disappointment on his face was too heavy for us to ignore, and Lewis Nkosi was recruited to play a white priest who had to be discoloured because of the attitudes of our country.

Bloke Modisane, *Blame Me on History*
(London: Thames and Hudson, 1963), p. 289-91

No-Good Friday's setting of Sophiatown backyards is in the main functional only: it permits the comings and goings of the comparatively large cast without straining credulity. Both this set and the interior of Willie's room of Scene 3 and 4 provide opportunities to show township aspirations for 'decent' living (in white terms) as being continuously frustrated by the class/race divisions of South African society. That is its meaning, somehow apart from the action: it shows black realities to whites, and in 1958 established the validity of black daily experience as subject matter for drama. The only image to transcend function is a sense of the vulnerability of the stage to tsotsis, which is part of that whole (maybe mythical?) communal life visible to the audience, and is contrasted diegetically through Willie's description of a white suburb (p. 126). The two indoor scenes permit more intimacy, yet Rebecca's most outspoken statements about her feelings for Willie are made to Guy, which dissipates the force inherent in a couple in the enclosed, almost claustrophobic space so common in Fugard and so telling in the bedroom scenes of *A Lesson from Aloes*. Except for the loneliness of Willie, facing his nemesis almost alone at the end, the play's explicit confrontations — with Shark and the tsotsis, the knifing of Tobias, even Rebecca's desertion of Willie — seem to raise no echoes from the stage space. A director would have to develop them all through grouping, movement, and colour.

Margaret Munro, 'Some Aspects of Visual Codes in Fugard', *English in Africa*, Grahamstown, XIX, No. 2 (Oct. 1982), p. 17-18

The fact that a multiracial team of pupils of Saint Barnabus College are producing Athol Fugard's first full-length play, *No-Good Friday*, for the first time in Johannesburg in nine years, is evidence of courage, but also of a consciousness of their history and their contemporary situation.

The play takes place in what used to be Johannesburg's black township of Sophiatown. Western Township, where Saint Barnabus is situated, is a part of what remains of the old Sophiatown. In the case of school performances it seldom happens that the surroundings and the situation portrayed on the stage are virtually the same as the surroundings and situation outside. This is probably one of the reasons why these young players are so convincingly able to live their roles. One has only the highest praise for Lucille Gillwald, the director, for the life she has blown into the eleven amateur players (of between the age of fourteen and seventeen).

For those who want to keep up with South African theatre history, this is a golden opportunity to see how meaningfully an early Fugard can be brought to life.

Leon de Kock, *Beeld*, Johannesburg,
27 March 1979, p. 8 (translated from the Afrikaans)

Nongogo

Two-act play in three scenes.
First production: Trades Hall, Johannesburg, 8 June 1959 (dir. Fugard; with Thandi Kumalo as Queeny, Sol Rachilo as Johnny, and Zakes Mokae as Blackie).
First British production: Crucible Studio, Sheffield, 27 Nov. 1974 (dir. Peter James; with Ena Cabayo as Queeny and Jimi Rand as Johnny).

Revived: Market Theatre, Johannesburg, 19 Nov. 1981 (dir. Lucille Gillwald; with Thoko Ntshinga as Queeny, Ramolao Makhene as Johnny, and Fats Dibeko as Patrick).
Published: Dimetos and Two Early Plays (1977).

The play is set in a shebeen or jazz honky-tonk bar off a busy street in Johannesburg in the 1950s. The shebeen-queen, known as Queeny, is now affluent, but needs to live down her past and her nickname, 'Nongogo' — a term used of a woman prostitute to be had for two-and-six, especially one who solicits mine-workers queuing for pay. Patrick, one of her maudlin regulars, acts as chorus, perpetually seated and sozzled, and his sidekick is 'Blackie', who slaves to keep the room respectable-looking. The essential story concerns smooth Johnny, the young salesman of knick-knacks, who cons Queeny by offering her a respectable married life and secure future. Through Sam he learns of her past and, unable to handle it, absconds, leaving Queeny broken with her regulars dispersed.

I can't agree with Athol Fugard's contention that the most positive contribution to South African theatre will come from non-whites ... and if he believes it, he must leave the business of writing plays to the Africans, for such work would have to be in the vernacular. I don't agree with other critics that his idiom and his language are unsuitable, that he should be writing in a *Cry, the Beloved Country* style — 'ah, my father, the white man's city has swallowed me up' would be embarrassing.

His play hooks us for the first two scenes because he presents a set of characters injured by circumstance, and psychologically wounded, struggling to find renewal. I don't agree that this can't happen to city Africans — as I have heard some complain.

Where Fugard's play falls short is in the denouement, when a fine situation is frittered away in a kind of ironical short-story ending. How much more compelling it would have been to have murdered the boy who almost became the shebeen-queen's saviour ... how much more bitter the climax.

The African players astonish by their untutored talents. We marvel at their skill in variety ... now we see it in the drama, unselfconscious, emotional, capable of depth.

Anonymous, *Sunday Times*, Johannesburg,
21 June 1959, p. 16

The Sheffield Crucible Theatre are completing their nine-week Athol Fugard season. . . . The most surprising thing about *Nongogo*, which opened last week, is its leisurely comedy. Set in a more than disreputable bar in the poor black quarter of Johannesburg, the play spreads itself in a thoroughly homely manner. Queeny and Sam, her slick protector; Blackie, her adoring, ferocious Quasimodo of a servant; Patrick, solemnly drowning his sorrows in cheap brandy while his wife is giving birth for the fifth time, are all sketched in with a loving, oblique realism of which Priestley would thoroughly approve.

Fugard is not a storyteller; he is a craftsman of situations. His plots often protrude like clumsy skeletons, and in his best plays he has done away with conventional plot altogether. His strength lies in the haunting resonances of confrontations. Like Beckett, he is a poet of inaction.

John Peter, *Sunday Times*, 1 Dec. 1974, p. 17

The Blood Knot

Full-length play in seven scenes.
Written: 1960, in conjunction with *Tsotsi* and early notebook entries, during and after a trip to Europe.
First production: Rehearsal Room of the African Music and Drama Association, Dorkay House, Johannesburg, Sept. 1961, then touring South Africa for six months (dir. Fugard; with Zakes Mokae as Zach and himself as Morris).
First London production: New Arts Theatre, Hampstead, 22 Feb. 1963 (dir. John Berry; with Ian Bannen as Morris and Zakes Mokae).
First New York production: Cricket Theatre, 2 March 1964 (dir. John Berry; with James Earl Jones and J. D. Cannon).
Revived: in a cut version, as *Blood Knot*, Yale Repertory Theatre, 17 Sept. 1985, transferring to Broadway (twenty-fifth anniversary of the original cast)
Published: Cape Town: Simondium, 1963; New York: Odyssey; Samuel French, 1963; in *New English Dramatists, 13* (London: Penguin, 1968); *Three Port Elizabeth Plays* (Oxford University Press; New York: Viking, 1974); *Boesman and Lena and Other Plays* (Oxford University Press, 1978); new version, as *Blood Knot*, in *Selected Plays* (Oxford University Press, 1987).

The play is set in Korsten black location, Port Elizabeth, in the 1950s — a wasteland including a polluted marsh — in the one-room shack (including sleeping space, cooking facilities and a table) of Zachariah. His lighter-skinned brother is Morris who, after trying to escape these conditions and 'pass' for white, has returned. The play is entirely a duologue between them, establishing the 'blood knot' of their interdependence, aggravated by the different roles assigned them outside in colour-bar South Africa. The plot hinges on Morrie applying for a pen-pal on Zach's behalf, her turning out to be white, her threatened visit, and her last-minute withdrawal. The evening games they play to mark time include fantasies of a happy family past, but lead to a climax where suddenly their aggressions release Morrie's curse on Zach, and Zach's near killing of Morrie.

In *The Blood Knot* Athol Fugard has written a very remarkable new play. It is remarkable not only for its content, but also because he, the author (like some of the New Wave playwrights of London) acted one of the two roles on Sunday night at a private showing with a power and conviction that held the audience enthralled for some three hours. The venue was the new Rehearsal Room of the African Music and Drama Association in Dorkay House which holds 120, and is severely limited in its facilities at present.

Stage setting was stark. But this is a stark play. The scene is a slum room in Korsten with two wooden frame beds on bricks, kitchen utensils on the side, and the back wall plastered with sheets of newspaper. Two men live in the room, and at curtain-rise one of them, Morris (Athol Fugard), is preparing the evening meal for the homecoming Zach, a job which includes a nightly footbath for Zach's calloused feet. Curiosity is immediately provoked by this odd ceremony, and the still odder relationship of the bearded, pale-skinned menial Morris to the Bantu-featured, yellow-skinned Zach, who manifestly resents the other's company.

In the morose clashing dialogue the situation emerges. These men are brothers, but Morris, with his lighter skin and Aryan features, can pass and has passed for white. Once he broke away and took to the road, and his thoughts, expressed in long soliloquies as he stares beyond the audience through a mesh of wire that represents a window, frequently return to the freedom and wonder of the hobo world where the colour of his skin was no bar.

New light breaks for Zach when Morris offers to find him a penpal, a girl, through an advertisement. This scene (there are seven in all) provides touches of humour and pathos and searing drama, too, when the girl Ethel, who strikes up a friendship, sends a photograph which shows she is white. All the bitterness and fears of Morris's divided personality are unleashed by this contretemps. A final twist to the agony is given when he is persuaded to stand-in for Zach and they spend their small savings to buy clothes to make him look presentable to meet the girl.

It is not possible to more than sketch out the savage irony with which the brothers play out their hopeless rehearsal for the meeting that will never take place. Mr. Fugard's own playing out of this tormented role was a tour de force. It is true he mistakes length for significance and that if he cut some scenes by half he would double their meaning. But for all its unwieldy length the play never flags. Even its literary patches are permissive, and some of them have the luminosity of real poetry.

Mr. Fugard's use of a Cape accent has a sour-sweet homeliness that carries it above caricature. There's a magnetism in everything he does — in the slyness, the sentimentality, the hopelessness, the rages, and the fears of his near-white dilemma. He has a valuable foil in Zakes Mokae as Zach, but the crux of the play remains Morris, the coloured man who is so near white.

Mr. Fugard's two earlier plays, *No-Good Friday* and *Nongogo*, had plenty of real meat in them. *The Blood Knot* is the finest so far. The problem is: where can such a play find a wider audience? Perhaps, like *No-Good Friday*, it will have to travel to Rhodesia, but its true home and greatest impact must surely lie here.

Oliver Walker, *The Star*, Johannesburg, 5 Sept. 1961

At regular intervals throughout Athol Fugard's *The Blood Knot* an alarm clock rings, summoning the actors to food or bed. Its jangle may also be welcome to members of the audience who find themselves, as I intermittently did, sunk in embarrassed sleep. . . . To some extent, I suppose, the piece reflects the guilt that the white South African feels about the Bantu. . . . Zakes Mokae is all tension, his lips stiffly furled, his neck muscles taut, and his vocal chords muted to a spasmodic rasp. American negroes act, sing, and dance with the finest: why is it, I wonder, that Negro artists who have lived under British rule are so painfully inhibited?

Kenneth Tynan, *The Observer*, 24 Feb. 1963, p. 17

For us in South Africa it is a hard-won freedom from the muzzling of thought and expression to get away with a production of, say, *Mother Courage* or Weiss's *Marat/Sade* play — even before segregated audiences. One had merely to watch the white audience, streaming in week after week to sit as if fascinated by a snake before Athol Fugard's *The Blood Knot*, to understand how in the theatre, as in perhaps no other medium, one can bring people face to face with those things in their society and themselves which they have long been conditioned not to think about.

Nadine Gordimer, *Contrast*, Cape Town,
III, No. 4 (July 1965), p. 54-5

I never cease to marvel at the stunning simple truth of James Baldwin's observation of what modern writing should be about. It is, he says, the effect people have one on the other which should concern artists, for without this the actions of their characters are meaningless. And in Athol Fugard's *The Blood Knot* (Theatre Royal, Brighton) there is evidence in plenty that this is so. Like Baldwin, this is a writer dealing with one of the burning social problems — that terrible term — of our time. Like Baldwin, he knows what it is like to live in a country where human beings are segregated, persecuted, and denied their rights by the biological accident of the colour of their skin.

And, again like Baldwin, he steadfastly resists any temptation to preach, to be precious, pious, or — being white — to patronize, in dealing with the subject which so obviously fills his heart with sorrow and indignation. He reduces it to terms of human beings. Plot and politics take second place in this finely woven dialogue.

Set in South Africa, the drama played out between the two characters on the stage here — one of whom is played by the author himself — gains its force and its fire always from the effects they have on each other. The awful implications of their actions are a secondary consequence. Mr. Fugard has, it is true, crystallized all the crass hypocrisy and inhumanity of the apartheid policies of South Africa by a very neat ploy. His two characters seem, when the curtain first rises, to be one white and one coloured. But, as the programme reminds us, the terms white and coloured in South Africa have very precise and legal meanings. The whole point of his analogy is that, different as their pigmentation may be, the two are in fact blood brothers.

It would have been so easy to go on from here and pump out meaningful propaganda about the ridiculousness of it all, to turn the whole play into a tract about the insidious evil which condemns a man to second-class citizenship not only for the shade of his skin but also his ancestry. For white as brother Morris might appear, in South Africa he is classed inescapably as coloured. Instead, Mr. Fugard delves deep into the psychology of their relationship. He probes the strengths and the weaknesses of the more sophisticated Morris and his bland, happy-go-lucky illiterate brother. He analyzes the effects the difference in their outward hue makes on their inner selves. It is startling and frightening. A chilling climax of unleashed brutality, with Morris playing the white man to Zach's 'black boy', resounds with unspoken questions.

We are left with a dreadful separation through colour and unbreakable tie through blood. It is, in miniature, the predicament of the human race divided by prejudices and joined by brotherhood in common humanity.

The performances of Mr. Fugard and Zakes Mokae fill the stage with throbbing life for the whole three acts. There are no clichés about their interpretations, just as there are none in the writing. Athol Fugard, with the nasal whine of the Afrikaner, shuffles around almost begging for forgiveness for the unexpressed shame he feels in his every moment, while Zakes Mokae, the fine natural man, sometimes displays the uncomprehending exuberance of a child, sometimes the pain of ancient sufferings.

This is a fine play, finely acted, and deserves to be seen. A thousand sermons could never make the impact this work does by its sheer art.

Jack Tinker, *Evening Argus*, Brighton, 17 May 1966

The Blood Knot is a surgical dissection of the two brothers; Fugard has stripped bare — tissue by tissue, layer by layer — two complex human beings. There are no dramatic events in *The Blood Knot*: except for the gradual revelation of the innermost beings of Morrie and Zach; inside the claustrophobic room, the playwright forces the two men to look deep inside themselves, and the vision of the abyss is as painful to them as it is to the audience. Magnetically and inexorably, Fugard's audience must live through these painful self-examinations; for this reason, a mere synopsis of Fugard's play does little justice to its terrifying intensity when experienced on stage. *The Blood Knot* shouts out to be acted because the drama of the play — both its tragedy and its comedy — is only perceived in the tempo and mood of the conversations between the two brothers; there are no stirring actions, but slowly and surely Fugard builds up the play to its final and dreadful climax when, in a scene of immense power, the two brothers are at last stripped of all their protective illusions.

Robert Green, 'South Africa's Plague: One View of *The Blood Knot*',
Modern Drama, Feb., 1970, p. 333
(on his own production, Dar-es-Salaam, 1967)

For English readers, of course, such dialogue as this has the added charm of genuinely conceived dialect drama, in which the familiarity of one's native tongue is distanced by those slight modifications of expression and emphasis which define the play's locale as precisely in verbal terms as its setting does in physical. Partly because of Mr. Fugard's gift for the colloquial, partly because of an occasional need for over-explicitness, the rapid exchanges between the brothers seem to work more convincingly than the lengthier speechifyings in which each is made to indulge. Or perhaps it is because the brothers, partners in a shared and comforting solipsism, only seem to have a rounded existence in relation to each other. It would be consistent with the play's conclusion to suggest that this is, indeed, the only meaningful reality which is to be permitted them: and it is certainly an awareness of such a reciprocal need that has driven Morris back to his brother's shack, an awareness captured by Mr. Fugard not in awkward retrospection, but in the natural course of verbal interplay.

Simon Trussler,
Introduction, *New English Dramatists, 13*
(Harmondsworth: Penguin, 1968), p. 13

New Haven, Connecticut. — When Athol Fugard's play, *The Blood Knot*, originally opened off-Broadway two decades ago, the author was hailed as a promising new voice from South Africa. That Mr. Fugard is now regarded as one of the world's finest dramatists, whose works probe the political tragedy of his native country in searingly human terms, is only one of many ironies evident in this twenty-fifth anniversary production.

Now in an outstanding revival at the Yale Repertory Theatre, the original cast — Fugard himself and the excellent black South African actor, Zakes Mokae — is reunited for the first time since a brief London engagement in 1966. The resulting production is, tragically, nothing if not more politically relevant today — a fact which loads much of the author's dialogue with even greater polemic urgency.

It is on the dramatic level, however, that Fugard's depiction of the human condition remains most impressive, sweeping beyond the shifting limits of any one nation. On the surface, the brothers' relationship is characterized by amiable fraternity — Zach works as park attendant while Morris keeps house at home. Underneath, theirs is an anguished battle for identity. As Fugard explains it in an author's note, this is an existential drama, exploring 'guilt about another's existence'. The final scene, in which the two coloured brothers play-act roles as white and black men, gives vent to the worst enmity among men. 'There you were spoiling my view and my chances', says Morris to his black brother. It is the kind of scene, culminating in the desperate query, 'Is there no other way?' that takes one's breath away.

Characteristically, *The Blood Knot* demands ensemble acting. Suffice it to say that Fugard and Mokae, who won a Tony Award for his role in *'Master Harold'*, are up to the task.

Hilary de Vries, *Christian Science Monitor*, 10 Oct. 1985

The Blood Knot

The remarkable critical attention given the 1986 revival of Athol Fugard's *Blood Knot* at the John Golden Theatre suggests a significance reaching well beyond the message or dramatic form of the play itself. Since the early 1960s, when *Blood Knot* made a lasting impact on the course of theatre in South Africa, Fugard has matured into one of the commanding dramatic voices in English. The enormous success of *Sizwe Bansi Is Dead* (1974) and *'Master Harold' . . . and the Boys* (1982) on Broadway established Fugard as that rare phenomenon, a political playwright whose plays transcend the politics that give them substance and dramatic life.

South Africa, like the Nazi holocaust, presents a human crisis whose vast proportions can easily overwhelm the encapsulated representations of the stage. In evoking a local reality so profoundly, Fugard's claustrophobic dramas reach both outward to universal human dilemmas and inward to South Africa's agonistic, all too human heart. *Blood Knot* clearly contains the seeds of this mature artistic vision, and Fugard's participation as both director and co-star in this production provides a unique insight into the author's conception of what his characters, his plays, and his country are all about. . . .

Zakes Mokae's Zachariah is the strongest and most penetrating interpretation of this character I have encountered. Black South African critics have often pointed to Zach as an example of what is lacking in Fugard's black characters: he is too stolid, too unconscious, too shuffling and dumb to represent them as a people. Mokae proves them mistaken. His Zach is aware of the uphill battle he must fight against Morris and what he represents, and he advances step by painfully logical step, like a climber driving pylons into the rocky face of an unforgiving mountain of racial myths. He plays his cards close to the vest, refusing to disclose more about himself or his intentions than is necessary as he lays his traps for the white beast in his brother. His stolidity is resistant; his unconsciousness, calculating; his dumbness, strategic. This is a man who speaks guardedly out of a refusal to lie, either to others or himself. With glacier-like immovability, he brings the weight of black experience and desire for self-determination to bear on the absurd fantasy and genocidal reality of apartheid.

As author and director, Fugard shares in the mastery of this performance, as well as that of his own. In this early, imperfect but passionate work and problematic production, Fugard gives us a unique insight into the origins of one of the most powerful social and moral imaginations of the English-speaking stage.

David Coplan, 'Retying the *Blood Knot*: Fugard on Broadway',
South African Theatre Journal, Johannesburg,
I, No. 1 (May 1987), p. 114-17

The Blood Knot

In *Blood Knot* John Kani (Zachariah) and Marcel van Heerden (Morris), with their flawless acting, show how warped the system of apartheid really is. The two actors continue the struggle which was started by author Athol Fugard and actor Zakes Mokae when the play was first performed at Dorkay House in Johannesburg in 1961. The man who was the 'third eye' on that day, Barney Simon, is steering them now, and the three are doing a marvellous job.

The Immorality Act, which has since been 'scrapped', was still in force then, forbidding sex across the colour line. In the play, that Act is shown to have been stupid, born out of fear that mixed marriages would spell the end of the white race.

The climax of the play is reached when an irritable Zachariah explodes because he has not seen his old-time friend, Minnie. And that leads to an examination of relations across various colour lines. *Blood Knot* is a lesson for all South Africans.

Victor Metsoamere, *The Sowetan*, Johannesburg,
19 Jan. 1988, p. 7

On a superficial level this play has dated — its most visible attack is on the Mixed Marriages and Immorality Acts. You know that, but you also know there must be a reason for reviving one of Athol Fugard's early works in 1988, so you look for the contemporary reality, the 'universal' that Fugard has always sought to sew into uniquely South African plays.

That they're not present in this production is the result both of deficiencies in the text and in the conceptualization of that text.

This is, above all else, a play about colour, about racial discrimination and prejudice on that level. But events and thinking in South Africa have moved well beyond isolating racism as the evil in this society and towards a position, now an orthodoxy almost across the spectrum of opinion, that racism was the tool first of subjugation and then of ideological justification for what has happened. Important though it is, it is a manifestation, a symptom rather than the real thing.

It might be argued that Fugard's play to some extent anticipates these developments. Morrie, who represents white society, controls Zach's savings, putting them away for a 'future' that will be economically secure. He is obsessed with order — an alarm bell announces Zach's return from work, supper, bedtime . . . but this constitutes only a small part of the work, neither sufficiently explored in the text nor teased out in this production.

To have the same impact as it did in the 1960s, *Blood Knot* should have been a play not about reality, or history, but specifically about the history of ideas. It was not, and this is perhaps a product of both Fugard's and Barney Simon's belief in the cathartic experience of theatre. The years have eroded the number of bogeys in this play that need catharsizing, and this continued emphasis robbed it of its potential to teach us about the way we used to think and used to conceptualize the conflict around us.

Within these limits Marcel van Heerden's performance was powerful, even compelling, as he struggled to capture the pain and tension of a bygone era. John Kani's, however, was undisciplined and soft — indulgent. His opening scene foot-massage was grossly hammed up — more like open-heart surgery without anaesthetic than a couple of calluses.

Historically this is an important play and a video should be kept in a national museum of theatre. But as part of the continuing and exciting development of South African theatre in the 1980s it seemed a rather regressive step.

John Campbell, *The Weekly Mail*, Johannesburg,
28 Jan. 1988, p. 21

Peter Cheeseman has directed a magnificent revival of Athol Fugard's first major play, *Blood Knot* (1961) at the New Victoria Theatre, North Staffordshire. It is the story of two Cape coloured brothers. Zach is dark, but by one of those cruel genetic tricks, Morris is almost white.

Zach does menial work at a factory gate, and Morris, since his unaccountable return a year before, keeps house. He lives for a future in which they will get away from the slum and make their own little farm in one of the blank areas on the map, a place where no one will notice them.

But Zach is hungry for adventure and for 'woman'. He lives in the present tense. The childhood they shared, in which Morris was his black mother's favourite, poisons the present. The past they don't share, when Zach had a friend and lovers, and Morris tried to be a white man, has left them both with shattered hopes. Bound together by the painful fact of blood, they cannot exist apart. They are almost lovers in their intimacy, and yet utterly different in temperament and language.

Gradually their common past is revealed until at the climax it becomes a burning reality. Morris urges Zach to take a female penfriend to sort out his burning libido. He pens Zach's letters (Zach can't read or write) and both brothers get deeply involved with the epistolary Ethel. But there's been a mistake: Ethel is a white girl.

Nothing could be more classical. Fugard rewrote the play in 1986 for the New York revival. He thought the earlier version 'monstrously overwritten'. He had learned the force of understatement.

Winston Crooke plays Zach, limping home, tall and almost broken. He is a powerful actor, his delivery sensitive of the volatile emotional situation, his diction impeccable. Gary Lilburn plays Morris, a white mouse of a man, terrified, sanctimonious, and vulnerable. Both are entirely credible. Under Cheeseman's direction, the hypnotic duet of *Blood Knot* is one of the high points of the autumn theatre season in the North. This vivid production should tour, and tour widely.

Michael Schmidt, *Daily Telegraph*,
22 Sept. 1988, p. 4

Hello and Goodbye

Play in two acts.
First production: Library Theatre, Johannesburg, 29 Oct. 1965
 (dir. Barney Simon; with Athol Fugard as Johnnie and Molly Seftel as Hester).
First New York production: Sheridan Playhouse, 18 Sept. 1969
 (dir. Barney Simon; with Colleen Dewhurst and Martin Sheen).
Revivals: King's Head Theatre Club, London, 22 March 1973 (dir. Peter Stevenson; with Janet Suzman and Ben Kingsley); The Space, 26 July 1974 — the definitive production, which also played at Riverside Studios, London, and was filmed by SATV and by the BBC (dir. Fugard, with Yvonne Bryceland and Bill Flynn)
Published: Cape Town: Balkema, 1971; New York: Samuel French, 1971; in *Three Port Elizabeth Plays* (1974); *Boesman and Lena and Other Plays* (1978); *Selected Plays* (1987).

A kitchen in a railway-worker's cottage in Valley Road, the poor-white quarter of Port Elizabeth (now demolished), in the depressed early 1960s. Johnnie is on guard, nursing his ailing father (who remains offstage), and expecting the return of his long-lost sister, Hester. Her arrival from Johannesburg signals a nostalgic reminiscence between the siblings, hinging on their resentments of parental control, particularly of their late mother's storing of all the good things in life in boxes. Johnnie maintains his dominance over Hester by pretending that their father is still alive, and Hester's unpacking of their heritage is a guilty search for the compensation money supposedly paid out to their father when he was crippled. Hester's discovery that their father is in fact dead and that she has been cheated leads to her return to her past way of life. Unreconciled to his sister, Johnnie — alone — assumes his father's crutches as his inheritance.

Hello and Goodbye

Far less inflammatory and thought-provoking than *The Blood Knot*, seen at the same Labia Theatre in February, 1962, this new two-character play by Athol Fugard has interest as a contribution to our indigenous drama but, in my opinion, is by no means the gem suggested in advance reports from Johannesburg.

For two people to hold attention in two acts for two hours is a formidable assignment, which can at times be accomplished through taut brilliant dialogue, at times by sheer power of performance. As much of Mr. Fugard's heart-felt writing is verbose, repetitive, cryptic, and self-indulgent to the author's needs, it rests almost entirely with the performance to broadcast his emotional wave across the footlights, which it certainly did last night to a large audience appreciatively tuned in for reception and applause.

If disconnected verbiage fills space left yawning through lack of action, Mr. Fugard packs it with such vernacular enthusiasm that we may accept it uncritically as authentic enough to the 'poor white' type represented on the stage in a welter of hate and bitterness.

They are a lonely man (Athol Fugard) with a wandering mind and his slovenly elder sister (Molly Seftel) who have not seen each other for twelve years till she returns to the 'second-hand' family home in Port Elizabeth from Johannesburg, where she has passed her time as a prostitute while he cared for their widowed father who lost a leg in a dynamite explosion.

Sensing that his sister has arrived with a scheme up her sleeve, the brother cunningly pretends indifference till shocked by the revelation that she is there to collect her share of the father's compensation money, amounting in her estimation to several hundreds of pounds.

In the first act the pair spar cautiously, with every sentimental — and inconsequential — detail of a frustrated past elaborated; in the second they fight in savage fury over the problems of the future, a future which seems to hold for him, at least, an ironic hope of 'resurrection'.

As the unfortunates for whom 'there wasn't enough of anything except hard times', Mr. Fugard and Miss Seftel offer an example of expert teamwork which our local so-called 'professionals' might study with reward, and prove that in this case, with no conscience to catch as in *The Blood Knot*, the players not the play are the thing.

Ivor Jones, *Cape Times*, Cape Town,
23 Nov. 1965, p. 7

As Johnnie, Fugard uncannily *is* the character. He skips and leaps, shushes his sister, is weakly cunning, and his head is as chaotically filled with stories and fragments of scripture and hackneyed old sayings and bits of ads as the second act floor is with rubbish. He is funny when,

Hello and Goodbye

after reading a detergent jingle, he mutters, 'Hell, they're blerry clever, hey?' but human-being-funny, not *Snoektown Calling* funny. For as an author Fugard has discovered something very obvious, that the mangled South African illiteracy is less a huge joke or a national snigger than a function of real human beings' lives. When he interpolates false poetry, he betrays that discovery, but many lines like 'a man on his own legs is a shaky prospect' (and there are dozens of them) not only read well — hauled through the thickets of a South African accent they emerge as a sign of a particular time and place and personality, and are consequently very poignant. It is almost like discovering a new language, this shock of discovery that the joke-patois of *Ag Pleez Deddy* is the language of people who suffer, are gay, and even in a subtle way insist on finding accommodation for their own dignity. Fugard has yet to stake everything on this — the moths-at-the-window sort of nonsense which flecked *The Blood Knot* has lessened but is still there — but with *Hello and Goodbye* he has shown what he can do, and already does it exhilaratingly, excitingly, and intensely.

Johnnie Smit is the first real English-speaking South African on the stage.

Anonymous, *Newscheck*, Johannesburg,
22 Oct. 1965, p. 33

Peter Stevenson's production is played by two of the RSC's finest actors, Ben Kingsley and Janet Suzman, who sink themselves unreservedly in the rhythms of desperation. Gesture alone conveys a great deal about their lives: Kingsley's solitary rituals before the sister arrives, and Suzman's arm gesture — as though throwing away something disgusting — and her businesslike nods of the head which suggest determination to get on with a task that has no meaning. After the revelation of the father's death she beats him to the ground with one of the old rags from the heap: then, exhausted, they subside into each other's arms. The embrace is only momentary: but the force of the show is that it presents past and present simultaneously, showing what they once were and what the conditions of Afrikaner white trash have made of them.

Irving Wardle, *The Times*, 23 March 1973, p. 11

Watching Athol Fugard's remarkable play, *Hello and Goodbye*, is the experience of plunging into all the undercurrents which make up the thoughtful man's feelings about South Africa and the South African's feelings about himself.

Vividly and painfully it assembles the vestiges of the Boer inheritance — the bull-like pioneering spirit, the rigidity of the Dutch

Hello and Goodbye

Reformed Church, the backward-looking, inbred thought of a society which has been sent to Coventry by the rest of the world. Fugard's is a unique voice crying from the wilderness; and, though one must not fall into the error of making a generalized statement about the Afrikaner (as indeed David Williamson's *The Removalists* has been taken by overseas critics as an accurate picture of daily life in Australia), it has the ring of truth about human nature as we can recognize it anywhere.

Hello and Goodbye is playing at the Australian Theatre, Sydney. First performed in 1965, it is set in a dilapidated house in Port Elizabeth, where a miner and his worn-out wife have brought up their son and daughter. The wife went early to her grave and as the play begins the husband is recently dead. Sitting at the table is the son, Johnnie, who has nursed his father for many years, ever since a charge of dynamite blew off his legs. The ghost of the old Boer, a helpless, maimed giant, dominates the play from the bedroom.

The old man is physically dependent, but his son is emotionally dependent. He is lost without his father because he has made no place for himself in today's world. Johnnie's loneliness is broken by the arrival of his elder sister, Hester, who returned her father's hate and by — as she says — whoring all the fathers, sons, and uncles of South Africa. She has returned to claim from her father her inheritance, which she believes to be the compensation he received for his accident, but which proves to be a junk pile of memories, only confirming that she is a whore and Johnnie is a cripple.

The process is not unlike that of Arthur Miller's *The Price* — but the hate and the maiming uncovered is not the selfish materialism behind the American dream but the degradation of a once-proud people whom the single-mindedness of colonialism has rendered impotent.

The play receives a very fine performance from Anthony Wheeler and Leila Blake, and is directed by Peter Williams. They act with the same passionate conviction with which the author himself projects what he believes. If I have a criticism, it is that all three are relentless in their demands upon the audience: an occasional lighter touch from the actors would be a welcome relief to the tension. But it is an extraordinary play which reverberates as all fine writing does.

Katharine Brisbane, *The Australian*, 8 Feb. 1974, p. 11

In the performances of Janet Suzman and Ben Kingsley at the King's Head in 1973, the play seemed overlong and less good than the same author's *Sizwe Bansi* or *Boesman and Lena*. That impression is totally reversed by Mr. Fugard's riveting production, visiting for three weeks from the Space Theatre in Cape Town. It emerges as a flawless piece of dramatic construction in which the search for the old man's money through boxes of family mementoes and discarded clothing is a central metaphor for investigating the past.

Mr. Fugard's language is richly poetic but never over-written. It is thrilling indeed to see Yvonne Bryceland — surely one of the great actresses of our time — and Bill Flynn rise to the demands of their text and inhabit the emotions and set speeches with such dazzling, confident assurance. With money, Hester would change her name and stay at a posh hotel. But riffling through the boxes she comes across her mother's dress and is momentarily transported to childhood by the lingering, familial smell. Miss Bryceland is briefly radiant at this point, before stifling her sorrow in the material itself. And when she returns from the inner room, Johnnie's secret discovered at last, she stands rooted to the spot for several minutes before unleashing an attack of throatily hysterical fury. This is acting of the highest order: powerful, controlled, unforgettable.

Michael Coveney, *Financial Times*,
1 March 1978, p. 15

Hester and Johnnie inhabit different worlds, but this brother and sister are alike in being wracked by loneliness and doubt. Each gropes despairingly to find some way of enduring an emptied, frustrated life and, as the action reveals, when they meet again in the family house each is so hemmed in by the resentments of childhood family enmities that they cannot meet in an understanding of their common suffering, much less find consolation or a life together. The parallels and contrasts between Hester, the physical prostitute, and Johnnie, the psychic cripple, are subtly interwoven as their encounter brings each to a species of self-recognition which is neither liberating nor strengthening. When Hester fails to find the compensation money paid to her father after his accident with the railways, and which she feels to be her due, her only recourse is to return, more defiantly and bitterly than before, to her life on the streets. Johnnie, relieved to be left to the solitude he fears, has no more to cling to than his father's crutches.

The patterning is strong but it never feels merely schematic, for the play moves with rhythms which give the unfolding encounter a naturalness and a variety of pace which keeps it lively and unpredictable. These rhythms are established mainly by the movement between monologues and dialogue in the play. And in this movement Fugard exploits to the full his capacity to show that speech often does not carry another's meaning to the listener so much as set up private resonances and associations. Hester and Johnnie can seldom exchange thoughts or feelings directly through their words for, apart from Johnnie's anxiety that Hester will expose the fact of his father's death which he cannot

The Coat

Play in one act, 'an acting exercise from Serpent Players of New Brighton, Port Elizabeth'.
Written: as scribe, from improvisations, 1966-67.
First production: privately, Port Elizabeth, Oct. 1967 (dir. Fugard; with three male and two female members of Serpent Players).
Published: Cape Town: Balkema, 1971; in *My Children! My Africa! and Selected Shorter Plays* (Johannesburg: Witwatersrand University Press, 1990).

Five performers on a stage bare of anything but chairs, with nicknames from plays they have recently performed (Lavrenti, Haemon, etc.), invite a 'white' audience to witness them devise a play which explains the conditions of life in New Brighton township in the 1960s, when the purge of political trials had removed many activists to Robben Island. The play hinges on the story of a coat, sent by a husband, sentenced to a long term, back to his wife. Torn between storing it or using it as instructed, the wife's story is followed through crucial scenes, each interrupted and discussed by the players. They contrive to force the wife into a drastic choice — the coat or food for her children — and then disband with the conclusion that for those who wait, that is also drama.

Parallel to work on his own plays has been that with Serpent Players. In 1963 he helped bring together this group from Port Elizabeth's African township of New Brighton. Men and women who worked all week as messengers, teachers, factory hands, servants, would meet with him when possible at night or weekends, to rehearse. . . . They survived in spite of an unimaginable accumulation of adversities: petty obstacles such as refusal of permits to Fugard to go into the township, and the difficulty of finding rehearsal places in Port Elizabeth; personal tragedies when, in the mid-sixties, among thousands of political arrests, one after another of the men in the group were imprisoned — the Azdak on the day of performance of *The Caucasian Chalk Circle*, the Haemon during *Antigone* — all for minor political offences such as attending a meeting of a banned African party some years earlier, and all ending up on Robben Island....

Revival came through Serpent Players' decision to do an actors' exercise: *The Coat*. During the trial of one of the actors, Fugard and this man's wife, Mabel, had attended court; Fugard to speak in mitigation of sentence (without effect). Afterwards, Mabel had been allowed to visit her husband in the cells. An old man there, who had just been sentenced to five years, grabbed her arm and, taking off his jacket, gave it to her and asked her to tell his family in the township what had happened to him and to give them the coat: 'Tell them to use it.' Now, with *The Messingkauf Dialogues* spurring them into improvisation and discussion, Serpent Players put together a script — the coat, its consequences and fate. One actor introduced it: 'Just before we start, let me answer any of you who might be asking, why the coat? Why not the man who wore the coat? Isn't a man a better subject? Yes, he would have been better, but you see it was *the coat* that came back.'

Mary Benson, 'Athol Fugard and "One Little Corner of the World",' *London Magazine*, XI, No. 6 (Feb.-Mar. 1972), p. 139-40

People Are Living There

Play in two acts.
First production: Close Theatre, Glasgow, 13 March 1968 (dir. Robin Midgley; with Carmen Silvera as Milly).
First South African production: Hofmeyr Theatre, Cape Town, 14 June 1969 (dir. Fugard; with Yvonne Bryceland as Milly and himself as Don).
First New York production: The Forum of the Repertory Theatre, Lincoln Centre, 18 Nov. 1971 (dir. John Berry; with Estelle Parsons).
Published: Cape Town: Buren, 1969; in *Boesman and Lena and Other Plays* (Oxford University Press, 1978).

The kitchen of an old, double-storeyed boarding-house in Braamfontein, Johannesburg, in the early 1960s — on a Saturday night, which is traditionally when whites go out for entertainment. Milly the landlady has been stood up by her lover of ten years. In retaliation she summons Don, the pasty-faced intellectual drop-out who lives in the backyard, to keep her

People Are Living There

company. Shorty the postman is stood up by Sissy, his wife, who goes out on her own. The three leftovers and lonely hearts generate a party to celebrate Milly's fiftieth birthday, which she forces into merriment when her lover appears. Sissy returns dissatisfied and hauls Shorty off to their unconsummated bed. Milly and Don, soul-mates, cannot come to terms with one another, but will die protesting at their neglect.

It's a serious indictment of South African promoters — their short-sightedness, perhaps, or their nervousness in the face of controversy — that a play such as *People Are Living There* should receive its world premiere in Glasgow, play in London, and then, more than a year later, be taken up for the first time in its country of origin. . . .

People Are Living There is something of a diversion for the playwright. It has an element of lightness which plays little part in his other work — and, in some ways, it is his most economical writing to date. In the past, and at his best, Fugard has shown a certain lyricism in his dialogue; at worst, something approaching a floridness of style. In *People*, though, I find a frugal and judicious Fugard at work, a writer capable of superb dialogue, almost Merceresque in his compulsion to make words fulfil their prime function: not merely to dazzle, but to communicate the essence of the theatrical situation.

In the production I saw at London's Mermaid Theatre in May last year, Robin Midgley, who directed, carried this economy through into both production and set. There it was simply an island of light, populated by four people and surrounded on all sides by black isolation. The actors, too, worked with a greater sparsity of movement; a more overt suggestion of their being trapped and frozen by their situation.

Fugard's own production, however, is considerably more detailed. He fears neither movement nor minutiae — Don, for example, poking holes through the crust on a condensed milk tin with a matchstick, while the others talk. . . .

Milly, the owner of the boarding-house (the landlord of it, as she describes herself), is the central character: it is her rejection, her defeat, her rallying and inordinate resilience that make her sympathetic. It is her fight to triumph over Ahlers, the unseen lover who has jettisoned her, that is the mainspring of the play. Yvonne Bryceland has on several occasions been remarked upon for her wide range and adaptability — but it is this part which provides the rare opportunity for her to reach for artistic height rather than mere technical breadth. . . .

Milly's character is protean, and Miss Bryceland is acutely sensitive to the delicate shadings of the part. Her transition into Milly's explosive

People Are Living There

rages, then back to the fragile passages where she reveals herself as she is, is effortless and controlled — a triumph of technique.

Athol Fugard as Don, Milly's confessor and judge, is detailed and correct. His is by no means an easy part; and it might well have flourished better had he not directed it himself. As the performance stands, though, it is at its best when Don is on the attack, the table-top psychologist, the digger into Milly's 'realism of the subconscious'.

Ken Leach's Shorty, while in the main well conceived, has its moments of inadequacy. Chiefly, I think, he is somehow too *physical* in the part to be completely convincing. The Shorty of the play boxes on Saturday night, it's true — but the muscularity, and some of Mr. Leach's mannerisms, make him more oafish than simple-minded, losing in the process some of the vulnerability and lovableness which make Milly's tearing into him towards the end that much more an act of brutality. . . .

Garner Thomson, *Cape Argus*, Cape Town, 16 June 1969, p. 13

The meek that inherit this earth, a quartet of half-educated English-speaking South Africans, bait and goad each other with truths and evasions — all the sorry tricks of human self-delusions and self-destruction — until most of what they have kept hidden is laid bare, exposed to your tender conscience as a humanitarian. It is beautifully done, with a subtle combination of cynicism and compassion that makes Fugard's method less cold and sinister than Pinter's, yet more immediate and relevant to everyday life than Beckett's.

The dialogue is marvellously garrulous and torrential, bubbling with more minute-to-minute invention than I recall from any of the earlier plays (going back to *No-Good Friday*); and Fugard's ear for the South African nuance — the turns of phrase that dot the speech of the half-Afrikanerized English-speaking South African — is unerring. In this he is extraordinarily well-served by his actors — particularly Yvonne Bryceland, whose performance in this role has been widely acclaimed elsewhere and proves, in the event, to have been even undervalued. . . .

Not only did she take one of them in ten long years ago as her lover (an unseen German who is now spurning her for an outside dalliance), but she has no false modesty about discussing him and his delinquencies with her other customers — a broken-down student at the University of Life named Don (Mr. Fugard), and a mentally retarded postman named Shorty (Ken Leach). Among these three the horrors of living are a source of endless discussion, of demand and response, and, ultimately, attack and reprisal, until their spiritual skeletons are laid bare — though not to rest.

Miss Bryceland dominates the stage with her vituperations and her sudden rallyings of embittered humour. It is a monumental performance, brilliantly observed in detail and using the South African accent with a kind of supple wrist-action that flicks the inflexions like a whip.

Mr. Fugard's acting is more familiar to us; it has the same edge and ardour for his point (as the playwright) as before. It is fine in this context, too, but it is as the playwright that he earns the highest laurels. If he lapses into self-conscious theatricalism, and sometimes into deplorably easy-won laughs (the off-stage rumble of a flushing lavatory, which I thought had gone out with red noses), he is still unquestionably this country's most accomplished and involved — humanly involved, that is — playwright.

Percy Baneshik, The Star, Johannesburg, 16 Jan. 1970, p. 11

People Are Living There cuts open a segment of domestic reality for us to watch four (really, three) people move through a night of their very ordinary lives. They sit around and smoke cigarettes and drink coffee and go to the loo. They have a party. Suddenly the whole thing explodes. These human beings, who have been indulging and humouring one another, only occasionally — and then gently — peeling a layer off one another's souls, suddenly abandon themselves to a violent exorcism, a savage Walpurgisnacht of traumatic group psychotherapy. What in the first act was a low-keyed version of *Virginia Woolf*'s 'Get the Guests' (but here directed against the landlady) becomes a pretty brutal exposé of her — and then, in turn, of other members of the menage.

But how thuddingly disappointing the ending is. It is as if Fugard suddenly lost faith in his play, as if he suddenly became aware that we would think it was 'a human story' (which it *is*) and that we would not think that clever enough.

Robin Malan, Teater SA,
Cape Town, I, No. 4 (Dec. 1969)

As an Afrikaans-speaker I have previously seen two productions of *People Are Living There*, and I was certainly stirred by the existential pain of the clapped-out characters in that Braamfontein boarding-house. But the Afrikaans version has now made me realize that nevertheless there was a certain distance kept between me and those English-speakers on the stage.

This is hard to describe, but it is as if the four figures in the piece now for the first time have become fully comprehensible *people*, while in the English text one way or another they stayed colourful *characters*. It also feels as if the Afrikaans which is filled with English expressions in this version is truer to the South African environment than the original English with its colourings of Afrikaans expressions and accents.

Perhaps my impression is very subjective, but for me . . . the Afrikaans colour that Fugard gives to his English is sometimes done as a slightly artificial way of romanticizing his characters as South Africans, of giving an unnecessary sculptural 'intimacy' to them.

Johan Bruwer, *Rapport*, Johannesburg, 29 Aug. 1982, p. 17
(translated from the Afrikaans)

The Last Bus

Short improvisation with Serpent Players.
First production: private performances, Port Elizabeth, March 1969 (dir. Fugard).
Unpublished, and unavailable.

Boesman and Lena

Play in two acts.
First production: Rhodes University Theatre, 10 July 1969 (dir. Fugard; with Yvonne Bryceland as Lena and himself as Boesman).
First New York production: Circle in the Square, 22 June 1970 (dir. John Berry; with Ruby Dee as Lena, James Earl Jones as Boesman, and Jakes Mokae as Outa).
First London production: Royal Court Upstairs, 19 July 1971 (dir. Fugard; with Yvonne Bryceland as Lena, Zakes Mokae as Boesman, and Bloke Modisane as Outa).
Published: Cape Town: Buren, 1969; New York: Samuel French, 1972; in *Three Port Elizabeth Plays* (1974); *Boesman and Lena and Other Plays* (1978); *Selected Plays* (1987).

The play is set on a bare stage representing the estuarine mudflats outside Port Elizabeth in the 1960s. The props are carried on by Boesman and Lena, two derelicts who have been evicted as squatters and who construct a shelter for the night. Their marriage is one of debasement and cruelty, caused by the hostile South African environment which processes them into human rubbish, by alcohol, and by the loss of their only child. Their camp-down is interrupted by a nameless black man (whom they call Outa), in terminal distress, seeking shelter. Boesman and Lena play one another over this intruder, who unnoticed dies in their midst. Boesman is convinced he will be held responsible for the death, and they decamp, their relationship restored only in so far as he has admitted his dependence on her.

They carry on their backs, in their arms, on their heads their entire worldly possessions and everything that justifies their existence.

Broken chairs, tin mugs, rusty pots, scraps of dirty clothing, old blankets are dumped each night in the open on the mudflats or the veld to be assembled into a makeshift shelter and picked up again to be trudged like some moving dustbin to another place the next day. . . .

Written with the grace of a poet and the vision of a man who loves and pities the broken and despised, this is easily the best play I have seen to come out of the troubled heart of Africa.

Milton Shulman, *Evening Standard*, 20 July 1971, p. 15

Boesman and Lena has no comfort for a supporter of apartheid. Lena, the coloured woman, has lost her pet mongrel, and befriends the old kaffir as a substitute; Boesman, who hates mongrels and kaffirs alike, is twice described as 'whiteman's dog, his tail between his legs, because the *baas* is going to be cross'. The idea is as explicit as that. Everyone but the white boss is someone else's dog, to be kicked or fondled or both; and there are times when the play's imagery has an even harder, angrier bite. 'Listen', cries Boesman, 'We're whiteman's rubbish. That's why he's so *beneeked* with us. He can't get rid of his rubbish. He throws it away, we pick it up. Wear it. Sleep in it. Eat it. We're made of it now. His rubbish is people.'

In South Africa it is the human being who is a form of urban pollution — a vexatious ecological problem to be cleared up by the bulldozer and dumped in some alien wilderness, far from white civilization. Could, and should, any artist be more direct with us than this?

Benedict Nightingale, *New Statesman*, 20 Aug. 1971, p. 247

When Lena wants to give Outa a mug of tea, Boesman spits into it, throws it in her face, and crawls away; she wipes her face and remarks to Outa: 'Maybe he'll sleep now.' Miss Bryceland is above praise as Fugard's characters are above pity or judgement. They exist; they are. It is easy to see why opponents and proponents of apartheid alike have found ammunition for their arguments in Fugard's writing: he tells the whole truth.

Charles Lewsen, *The Listener*, 29 July 1971, p. 157

Boesman and Lena

Undoubtedly Mr. Fugard presents us with a memorable image of the human degradation engendered by a racist regime: his central figures are like a Cape Coloured Didi and Gogo doomed to spend the rest of their life together, eternally bickering in the void. There is also a raciness and vitality in the dialogue with its unfamiliar Afrikaans diction and speech rhythms. But in the end it seems to me not quite enough for the white liberal dramatist to offer his coloured contemporaries his pity, his compassion, and his despair. What surely is needed, in the context of South Africa, is an affirmation of the fact that that country's tragedy is man-made and therefore capable of change: in short, some political gesture. The trouble with Mr. Fugard's play is that, while deploring the status quo, it also unwittingly helps to reinforce it.

Michael Billington,
Plays and Players, Sept. 1971, p. 49

I understand Lena. I relate to her particular reality because it is mine and every black woman's. I can understand the extent of her poverty and her filth and absolute subjugation. I know what it is to be denied my rights as a citizen and as a human being. To me, Lena is more than a woman and Boesman is more than a man. On one level they represent the universal struggle of black against white, man against woman. But they are also victims of something that is permeating an entire culture, and if we're not careful, it could happen to us. *Apartheid*. And starvation and brutalizing of the human spirit. There is deliberate up-to-date genocide going on in South Africa right now, but it's not publicized because the United States and Germany and even Japan have so much money tied up there. And in spite of this oppression, Lena and hundreds of others like her still struggle to exist. Lena can even fight to replenish her spirit right there in that stinking African mudflat. She can still find a momentary joy with a dying old kaffir because when she tells him her wretched life story, the act of telling it reaffirms her will to live. Lena never feels sorry for herself, you understand. She has gone beyond life's pain to a point where she must demand certain things for herself, and when she does demand something from Boesman, she stops being afraid.

I have always been reticent about expressing myself totally in a role. But with Lena I am suddenly, gloriously free. I can't explain how this frail, tattered little character took me over and burrowed so deep inside me that my voice changed and I began to move differently. Yet I am in control too. It is all very strong and magical and I'm alive with her as I've never been on stage.

Ruby Dee, interviewed by Patricia Bosworth,
'Every Black Woman is Lean',
New York Times, 12 July 1970, p. 1

Suddenly, the most amazing things begin to happen in this play which Walter Kerr said has no movement (!!!). When Lena defies Boesman, when she stops holding on for dear life to the bits and piece of life, when she lets it all go, when she dies to her fears . . . on the very *instant*, Boesman's power over her comes to an abrupt end. Before our eyes, a slave dies and a person is resurrected. It is given to Lena, the woman, to embody the Christian-Freudian perception that one dies by drowning oneself in the sea of one's fears, and is re-born with the power of self-possession.

Boesman, humbled by Lena's new majesty, capitulates utterly. In a litany of penance, he recites the history of their wanderings. . . . She understands, even as we do, that the litany is the plea of a really terrified man, and, of course, in her new strength, she is infinitely merciful . . .

It is a great play, and Ruby Dee gives the performance of her life. Every woman in New York should see it.

Vivian Gornick, *Village Voice*, 23 July 1970, p. 55

Boesman and Lena is the kind of play that 'nobody' writes any more, representational, sequential, mimetic; but it is rooted in such a felt need, its symbolism is so thoroughly assimilated, its tragic view so whole-souled, that it again proves a sometimes forgotten truth: no art form is dead so long as it fits the purpose of a committed and talented artist. There are at least two ways in the theatre to reach the elemental: by going forward from the moribund present or by going back from it. In formal terms, Fugard has done the latter.

Stanley Kauffmann,
New Republic, 25 July 1970, p. 25

'Your words are just noise, nonsense', Boesman says to Lena. In Athol Fugard's play, Field Day's fourth annual production, Lena is a middle-aged black woman existing in the wasteland of apartheid, so peripheral to the white man's society that it is difficult for her even to make sense. She talks incessantly but is in reality voiceless. Boesman, her man, sees things more clearly than she does but understands even less. We meet them, these two displaced people, homeless in every sense, on the dried-out mudbank of the Swartkops River, where they have come after the demolition of their shack by white officialdom. . . .

Boesman and Lena is . . . a superb play, and by and large Clare Davidson's production sticks close to Fugard's text, avoiding the risks that any attempt to relocate the action nearer home would entail. Stephen Rea's Boesman and Deirdre Donnelly's Lena exist somewhere between straightforward naturalistic portrayals of South African blacks and slightly distanced comments on the characters. The actors are white and Irish, the accents are South African, and the mannerisms black.

For Lena, the past is so fractured, so rootless, that she has difficulty convincing herself that she actually exists in the present. She is, as Boesman taunts, 'stupid from yesterday's wine', disorientated by the unreality, the lack of real human contact, of her personal history. When an old, dying 'kaffir' wanders into proximity she seizes on him as a way of confirming that she is here and that the time is now, a way of capturing a moment, however fleeting, of personal validation. She has the courage for once to defy Boesman, though we know that in the end he will tire of her incessant chatter and lapse into mute survival....

There is a vivid savagery in Stephen Rea's Boesman and a pleading desperate selfishness in Deirdre Donnelly's Lena that carry great conviction. Rea plays a man trying to forget his humanity, taking refuge in animal gestures and movements; Donnelly a woman trying to remember her humanity, tentative in her movements, probing and searching. They combine into an emotional blowtorch, stripping away the comfortable familiarity of pain and humiliation to suggest the crumbling residue of self-awareness beneath.

Desmond McAleer's Wabatutu, the dying Bantu who sits with Lena through the night, is full of darkness and unspoken sorrow.

Finlan O'Toole, *Sunday Tribune*, Dublin, 25 Sept. 1983, p. 7

Friday's Bread on Monday

Sketches of life in New Brighton, based on improvisations with Serpent Players.
First production: private performances, Port Elizabeth, 15 Oct. 1970 (dir. Fugard).
Unpublished, and unavailable.

Friday's Bread on Monday *was built mainly on mime. The half dozen actors trooped onto the stage and sat on chairs back right. After the audience had set up an expectant silence, Nomhle Nkonyeni rose, came forward, fell to her knees, and started an absolutely convincing — but not realistic — mime of rising at four a.m. and mobilizing her family. In one of the few pieces of dialogue in the piece she addresses her imagined son and dispatches him to buy last Friday's stale bread. She then rouses her sullen husband (played by Winston Ntshona) and tries to bring him to recite the morning Lord's Prayer. His gullet sticks at 'Give us this day our daily bread' and he storms out to walk to work. Nomhle is left alone and the four remaining actors, still sitting, start a hollow clapping which the audience is dared-and-not-dared to take up.*

This clapping begins and ends each subsequent piece and sets up a profound discomfort in the audience. On occasion, when the mime in a particular sketch is good, the audience claps back — but the hollowness of the stage clapping remains. The play proceeds through a wonderful, gibbering piece of rubbish-bin scavenging by John Kani, a delicately comic bus-queue passage involving the men, and a violent piece of prison mime to the climax, which is, oddly enough, merely the walk to work of Winston Ntshona. As he walks-on-the-spot, John Kani, sitting back right, gives an ironic commentary on his bravery and doggedness, his cowering before a pass-hunter and his final arrival, late, at work.

The burden of the play was, as I took it, that the 'inheritors of poverty' cannot solve their continually revolving problems by simple goodness, devotion, or generosity to one another.

Rob Amato, Sketsh, Johannesburg,
No. 1 (July 1972), p. 17

Orestes

A one-act experiment in theatre.
Written: as scribe, in collaboration with performers of the Cape Performing Arts Board Theatre Laboratory.
First production: Castlemarine Auditorium, Cape Town, 21 March 1971 (dir. Fugard; with Yvonne Bryceland as Clytemnestra, Wilson Dunster as Orestes, and Val Donald as Electra).
Published: 'Orestes Reconstructed: a Letter to an American Friend', *Theatre Quarterly*, VII, No. 32 (1979); in *Selected Shorter Plays* (1990).

Set in a bare space in-the-round, with only a bench and a chair. The three performers represent two sets of triangular relationships: Clytemnestra, Orestes, and Electra; and the mother and daughter killed by John Harris, the protester who left a bomb in a suitcase in the Johannesburg station concourse in the 1960s as a gesture of defiance against apartheid laws. Key moments from the one myth (the violence of Clytemnestra killing her husband, enacted as the actress dismembering the chair) overlap into the other (the mother and daughter on the bench being blown up). A virtually wordless script, depending on mime-games, culminating in a statement by each performer at the end about the vocabulary of drama.

They've been working behind closed doors for two months now, and the names of Fugard and Bryceland, which featured prominently in 'old' theatre last year, hold enough public appeal for there to be a natural curiosity about their activities....

In all fairness, I must confess that my initial reaction to watching Wilson Dunster playing trains, or Val Donald building sand castles, was one of utter bewilderment.

What we saw was an exercise in concentration and a set of drama techniques of varying quality, in which the three artistes 'told' the story of John Harris, who was hanged for exploding a bomb on Johannesburg station seven years ago.

There is a minimum of dialogue and the props are a bench, a chair, and a suitcase. The exercise is presented in-the-round.

It seems fairly obvious that Bryceland is getting something valuable from this experiment that she *believes* in. Let us hope the other members of the company are enjoying a similar experience.

Terry Herbst, *Cape Times*,
30 March 1971, p. 8

Most of my misgivings about Athol Fugard's 'experiment perilous' evaporated at this second viewing last night. I found myself involved and excited, even moved — and this experience seemed to be shared by the greater part of the audience.

I make no apologies for my earlier lack of comprehension. My experience then was as valid as the one I had last night. Should I see *Orestes* again — and time and opportunity willing, I intend to — who knows? My reactions may be quite different again. This is in keeping with the nature of the project.

Of course the work has changed considerably since I saw it in Cape Town. Much of the original material has been drastically pared down; some of it has been discarded altogether. There has been a degree of elaboration and some new material has been added. No doubt the present shape is not the final one. The author and players must continue to search for more expressive means to put their message across. Ideally, the audience should search with them. But, as it stands, the work is eloquent for all its sparsity of dialogue.

Two youthful figures — as yet they have no names — play games of discovery, while the mother figure — the Clytemnestra of myth — looks on. The mother suffers birth pangs, calls out in anguish for her lost child (Iphigenia, sacrificed by Agamemnon), then symbolically destroys the murderer by smashing a chair.

The Orestes figure is confined in a cocoon. He is the White South African and must grope blindly for his justification. He makes a savage protest against the guilt of society, but violence breeds violence and a woman dies. Yes, says the Electra figure to the lost, bewildered mother, I do know the Paul Jones. . . .

The performers are strong and arresting. Yvonne Bryceland is the Clytemnestra figure — a primeval maternal force, relentless in defence of her young. Wilson Dunster is the Orestes-John Harris figure, confused instrument of a revenge more terrible than he imagined. Val Donald is Electra, the instigator, at once innocent and all-knowing.

Raeford Daniel, *Rand Daily Mail*, Johannesburg,
27 Apr. 1971, p. 8

In part influenced by Grotowski's *Towards a Poor Theatre*, in part the result of his own creative development, in 1971 Fugard set out to produce theatre not dependent on written text, and thus free to exploit non-verbal imagery: visual images, images of rhythm, imagistic juxtapositions that do not demand the response of intellectual mediation. The few words of 'text' served mostly to identify and label, hardly ever to express directly the interrelationships between characters. Characters were not rounded, not 'studied' in the conventional sense — they too were reduced to an overlaid series of images. One actor was at once John Harris and Orestes; another was Clytemnestra destroying Agamemnon physically through the image of the demolition of a chair, and at the same time she was the old-woman victim of the bomb. . . .

The richness of Aeschylus' net of causation and motivation was chosen to underlie the figure of Clytemnestra; his Orestes and Electra Fugard drew from Euripides' stark, emotionally committed pair. It is important to realize that Fugard was not interpreting Aeschylus or Euripides: he merely juxtaposed, or rather superimposed, like a double exposure in photography, so that one perceived two images which fused to make a new pattern. Because the images were primarily visual, they did not even evoke an intellectual response (and did not demand an intellectual preconditioning). They drew a deeper response from the emotions, and thus perhaps came close to a genuinely mythopoietic experience.

E. A. Mackay, 'Antigone and Orestes in the Works of Athol Fugard', *Theoria*, Pietermaritzburg, No. 74 (Oct. 1989), p. 31-2

Statements after an Arrest under the Immorality Act

Full-length play.
Written: for the opening of the fringe theatre The Space, Cape Town.
First performance: The Space, Upper Long Street, 28 March 1972
   (dir. Fugard; with Yvonne Bryceland as Frieda and himself as Errol).
First London production: as part of a 'South African Season' including *Sizwe Bansi Is Dead* and *The Island*, Royal Court, 22 Jan. 1974 (dir. Fugard; with Yvonne Bryceland and Ben Kingsley).
First New York production: Manhattan Theatre Club, 5 Feb. 1978
   (dir. Thomas Bullard; with Veronica Castang and Robert Christian).
Published: Statements (Oxford University Press, 1974).

This play follows a non-linear chronology of fragments past and present of a love relationship between a 'man' and a 'woman'. She is Frieda Joubert, the (white) librarian of a Karoo town, and he is Errol Philander, the (classified 'coloured') local schoolteacher. The setting is the floor of the library in the stacks, where they have been meeting in secret, but is also the interrogation room of the police station where they are harassed and forced to confess their 'guilt' under the South African law of the day prohibiting mixed-race sex. The lovers have only blankets to cover themselves and are caught nude together by police photographers who punctuate the action. Their guiltless monologues interweave beautifully, interrupted by the banal and passionless indictments of the law, in the person of Detective-Sergeant J. du Preez.

I want just to deal with what I call the 'allegory of naming'. Bontrug. Why Bontrug? This is part of the resonance that we have. Errol Philander, the coloured teacher, and Frieda Joubert, the white librarian, have an affair and they are arrested under the Immorality Act. Only

Statements after an Arrest

those people who have lived in those townships for coloureds know the names that are given there. Bontrug could be beautiful, and it could just possibly be negative. Yet here are both meanings, cheek by jowl, black and white. What is all this about? By using these names, Fugard is dealing with the immorality of an act which is called the act against immorality. When he has Philander talk about his life and tell how he must walk to work through a little ditch filled with shit, then I see the relevance of 'It's all political'. This is where we can see the moral dimensions of a play. Where you have to eat, where you have to sleep, how you have to sit, where you may stand — all this is included in Fugard's play, *Statements after an Arrest under the Immorality Act*.

Cosmo Pieterse, speech delivered at the
African Studies Association Conference,
Austin, Texas, March 1972,
Issue, VI, No. 1 (Spring 1976), p. 49

It is notable that the most resonant speech in the play is delivered by Miss Bryceland, when under interrogation, *about* her body. It is a strange and horribly affecting mixture of pride and abasement (with an admixture of simple shyness); in the delivering of it, Miss Bryceland becomes extremely beautiful, the culmination of a process that has been at work all evening. It consists of looking at a woman's body, accepting it for itself rather than as a dream object, and coming to value it. In fact, we have here something very rare: a dramatization of love. In achieving this, Mr. Fugard, without any explicit denunciation, has said all that essentially needs to be said about South Africa's racial laws.

Robert Cushman, 'The Naked Truth',
The Observer, 27 Jan. 1974, p. 14

It is an implicit assumption throughout the play that there is something beautiful in the idea of a white woman disrupting a coloured home, and either deceiving a coloured wife, or inflicting on her pain and anguish.

I insist upon this because Mr. Fugard tells his story in a series of reminiscent conversations which Frieda and Errol have with each other after intercourse. Thus Errol's wife, never being seen, is too easily forgotten. Yet she is vital to the way in which the intrigue between her husband and the white woman should be regarded. The play is a protest against an immoral Act; but it is itself immoral.

Harold Hobson, *Sunday Times*,
27 Jan. 1974, p. 17

Sizwe Bansi Is Dead

A full-length, workshop-devised production.
Written: in collaboration with John Kani and Winston Ntshona, inspired by a conversation with John Kani in 1968.
First production: The Space, 8 Oct. 1972 (dir. Fugard; with John Kani as Styles/Buntu and Winston Ntshona as Sizwe Bansi).
First London production: in repertory with *The Island*, Royal Court Theatre, 20 Sept. 1973 (dir. Fugard; with the original cast).
First New York production: in repertory with *The Island*, Long Wharf Theatre, 10 Oct. 1974 (dir. Fugard; with the original cast).
Published: in *Statements* (1974); *Sizwe Bansi Is Dead and The Island* (New York: Viking, 1976).

The setting is Styles's Photographic Studio in New Brighton, Port Elizabeth, and the time is always updated to be the day of performance — in fact, the action is derived from the day's newspaper headline. Styles controls the entire play, waiting for customers to be photographed, and catering willingly to all their pride and self-delusions. The first half is a monologue by Styles, explaining directly to the audience how he came by the studio, having escaped the worker's life at the Ford factory, stressing his spirit of 'free enterprise'. When one customer knocks to interrupt him, the inserted play of 'Sizwe Bansi' occurs, as one possible case history of the photographer's day. In the play within, the character wishing to be photographed tells his story up to that moment: how as a work-seeker in Port Elizabeth, without a pass and the necessary permit, he has been sheltered by Buntu (played by Styles) who 'fixes' that his photo be swopped on a dead man's pass: thus he may either lose his real name and assume that of Robert Zwelinzima to gain employment to support his family back in the Ciskei — or stick to his name and die. Living with this false identity, he is for a while secure, and wishes to send his wife a 'happy snap' to reassure her about his success. The piece concludes with the photo taken by Styles back in the studio.

Theatre, as these actors conceive it to be, is not a separate structural entity, divorced from the empirical here and now, but an opportunity for the close scrutiny of immediate realities. Thus the audience, as well as the actors, must be 'used' since they too have a part to play — and it is not one of passive acquiescence in an evening's entertainment.

White audiences, under any circumstances, would tend to be suspicious of demonstrative audience participation; and when invited to respond wholeheartedly and without inhibitions to the plight of a black man entangled in the nightmare of influx control, reactions can only be complex. These actors, therefore, have to exert all of their considerable warmth and charm to elicit a little restrained empathy.

The first 30 or 40 minutes of the 'play' are devoted to the task — and it is a tricky one — of breaking down the audience resistance: the old ingrained habits, that is, of passive attention, polite applause, and an expectation of 'forgetting' oneself for a couple of hours. The tone of the opening half of *Sizwe Bansi*, then, is light, humorous, vivacious. After some moments of wondering when the actual 'play' is going to begin, one begins to realize that it never will, in *that* sense.

Jean Marquard, *To the Point*,
Johannesburg, 23 Dec. 1972, p. 46

If *Sizwe* is to the black people a record of their misfortunes, then well and good, it succeeds in recording these. They (blacks) were certainly happy with the way these records have been kept. In other words, they were entertained throughout. But if it was also an occasion to stimulate them to some positive thinking about their lot, I doubt if this was done. They laughed too hard at the white man to see beyond that point. I doubt whether the black audiences saw the successful portrayal of the black servant by John. I hope they dismissed, like I did, his advice about adapting oneself to the requirements of the moment. Winston as Sizwe can't be a man if he gives up his name to avoid starving in the Bantustans. That starvation he must face to become a man and retain his pride as a man! For me this is what is meant by sacrifice — which many of us have forsaken for the comforts of the day!

Sipho Sepamla, *Sketsh*, Johannesburg,
Summer 1973, p. 24

The technique of the open space theatre with its minimum of props is a good choice for *Sizwe Bansi Is Dead*. The action takes place in the mind of one man whose memories and associations take us from a factory to a photographer's studio, from a private house to a crossroad, and the stage adapts easily to these quick changes. The play takes the form of one long monologue in which the main character tells us what happened to him and some of his friends. We are presented with a random slice of his experience, selected according to the principle of associations, and prompted by an article in the newspaper which the actor is reading when the play starts. The dramatic monologue is particularly well suited to the subject. The actor picks out a member of the audience and pretends to have an informal and honest heart-to-heart talk with him. This avoids the declamatory aspect of the soliloquy, and together with the small bare stage it creates an atmosphere of intimacy which forces the social criticism away from the pompous or the didactic.

Kirsten Holst Petersen,
'The Problem of Identity in a South African Context',
ACLALS Bulletin, Mysore, No. 1 (1974), p. 13

The main reason it is satisfying is because it tells us things we don't know, or haven't bothered to imagine, about the epitome of our worst fears, the world's most totalitarian state.

For me, the political value of *Sizwe Bansi Is Dead* doesn't reside in the moral slant of its documentary content so much as in the formal innocence with which the content is presented. Like so much good popular art, it demonstrates that neither the old forms nor the modernized ones are as feeble as we post-European ironists sometimes believe. Created by black Africans under the guidance of a post-European, the play has the kind of freshness that gave the novel its name.

Robert Christgau, *Village Voice*, 19 May 1975, p. 94

There emerge two contradictory messages in the play: a cry of outraged human dignity stemming from the indignities of the urban situation confronting Sizwe Bansi (a cry echoed in Styles's earlier commentary on his work routine at the factory) and a plea for patient endurance on the part of Styles the photographer, a plea which at moments does not escape the charge of complacency. The nature of these contradictions is inevitable, for they are embedded in the liberal position itself. The cries of outrage against the alienating conditions of the South African wage-labour system have to be balanced against the more persistent voices of accommodation. Contradictions also occur *within* the fragmented consciousness of individual characters such as Sizwe and Styles, who contain within themselves different and opposing voices.

Sizwe, in contrast to his customary tone of patient perplexity, does make one direct appeal to the audience for sympathetic understanding of his simple, indeed simplistic, plea: the right to urban employment and identity. The questions he puts to the audience are purely emotional appeals to 'man's better nature', a key concept in liberal philosophy, which at this point in the play manifests itself as an undefined existential assumption to be shared by actors and audience. Audiences are 'involved' [only] to the extent that they are asked to 'feel' for the plight of Sizwe and participate in an emotional and abstract ritual of idealized liberal brotherhood.

Hilary Seymour,
'*Sizwe Bansi Is Dead*: a Study of Artistic Ambivalence',
Race and Class, XXI, No. 3 (1980), p. 284-5

The venue was Saint Stephen's Hall in New Brighton, Port Elizabeth, and the occasion was our first public performance of *Sizwe Bansi Is Dead* in a black township in South Africa. Date: September, 1974. The play was already nearly two years old, but it was only after its West End run that we felt sufficiently protected by its overseas success to risk the hazards involved in a township performance. Up until then its life in South Africa had been restricted to private performances before invited audiences, circumstances which theoretically made us safe from censorship and police interference.

I have never yet known an audience that responded to the first half-hour of the play as if it wasn't getting its money's worth of laughter. New Brighton was more than just 'no exception'. They knew in a way that no previous audience had known the finer nuances of what John was talking about and could recognize and celebrate every local reference.

Listening to them, however, I couldn't also help feeling that something more than just a response to a brilliant comedy performance was involved. What Brecht says of crying and lamentation in his *Messingkauf Dialogues* applies equally to the gale of laughter that was sweeping through Saint Stephen's Hall that night. It was the sound of 'a vast liberation'. To take still further liberties with 'poor BB': New Brighton was mixing laughter into an account of the blows it had received. It was making something out of the utterly devastating.

Argument and counter-argument, angry declarations and protests, followed fast and furiously. As I stood at the back of the hall listening to it all I realized I was watching a very special example of one of theatre's major responsibilities in an oppressive society: to try to break the conspiracy of silence that always attends an unjust social system. And most significant of all: that conspiracy was no longer being assaulted just by the actors. The action of our play was now being matched and equalled by the action of the audience. People were saying directly and forcefully, almost recklessly so, what they felt and thought. If the police had been present I'm sure that would have been the moment when they would have decided to act.

Fugard, 'When Brecht and Sizwe Bansi Met in New Brighton',
The Observer, 8 Aug. 1982, p. 31

The Island

Full-length, workshop-devised play.
Written: as a companion piece to *Sizwe Bansi Is Dead*, in collaboration with John Kani and Winston Ntshona, using the names 'John' and 'Winston' as characters. Originally entitled *Die Hodoshe Span*.
First production: The Space, 2 July 1973 (dir. Fugard; with John Kani and Winston Ntshona).
First London production: Royal Court Theatre, 12 Dec. 1973 (dir Fugard; with the original cast).
First New York production: Edison Theatre, 13 Nov. 1974 (dir. Fugard; with the original cast).
Published: in *Statements* (1974); *Sizwe Bansi Is Dead and The Island* (1976).

The piece begins and ends with lengthy, backbreaking mimes of hard labour in the Robben Island maximum security prison for political offenders. Two 'political' prisoners are pitted against one another, each filling the hole the other is digging. Back in their joint cell, 'John' and 'Winston' show that their solidarity is unbroken by this severe torture, and before lights-out they play games, remembering their families. The news comes that the appeal of one of them has succeeded and so they are to be divided soon. Most of their activity is geared towards presenting a two-man version of Sophocles' Antigone *at the prison concert, and the last scene uses us as audience: Creon's case for law and order is opposed by Antigone, who pleads humanity and willingly accepts incarceration as an act of defiance against tyranny. They are returned to hard labour to do their now-different times.*

It was called *Die Hodoshe Span*, Afrikaans for a work team under the supervision of Hodoshe (the carrion-fly), an infamous senior warder at Robben Island. Taking as its theme two men who had got themselves into trouble and had been sent to Hodoshe, they created a work about brotherhood and the human spirit's ability to survive.

During those fourteen days of playmaking, dealing with an issue that so deeply affected their lives, the tensions grew among the three. Fugard would ask a question and Kani and Ntshona would ask each other: 'If Athol could ask a question like that, maybe he doesn't understand us as we thought he did'. Kani says, 'Athol is a white man in South Africa. John and Winston are black men in South Africa. Sometimes it is difficult or even impossible for us to understand what operates in those little white boxes. And we fought, and we got very mad and yelled and cried.

'Then Athol told us to quit for a while and we all sat down and cooled off. Then after a long while he said to us: "You know what? If ever we decided to stop acting and to do something else instead, we would still need to be cool and not self-indulgent with passion. Because whatever you do — not only as in making plays — takes care and patience, not anger."

'You see, Athol taught us that we need our art, not propaganda. We tell a story in the simplest form and then we add art to the telling of it. Athol always reminds us that the story is enough and the message will take care of itself. The truth is bigger than ourselves and we should tell it as simply as possible.'

John Kani and Winston Ntshona, interviewed by Peter Rosenwald, 'Separate Fables', *The Guardian*, 8 Jan. 1974, p. 10

Creon's explanation of his *Realpolitik* might have come from today's newspapers, but it is Antigone, in her absurd straw wig and primitive falsies, who is the core of the play. Her defiant acceptance of her fate — to be walled in until death rather than leave her brother dishonoured and unburied, as carrion on the battlefield — has a heartrending poignancy.

Like previous works by Athol Fugard and his actors, *The Island* is an assertion of humanity rather than a play. It dares to proclaim that dignity and nobility can transcend oppression and degradation. Few of us are qualified to judge it; we can gaze at it in wonder and awe and humility and express our gratitude.

Frank Marcus, *Sunday Telegraph*, 6 Jan. 1974, p. 16

It is very difficult in these two plays to apportion praise. John Kani, who is short and thin and quick, and Winston Ntshona, who is big and solid and slow, are quite exceptionally good actors. Athol Fugard is well-known as a playwright and director. Just how the three of them came to decide how each scene should go, only they can tell. But it was generally felt that these two plays were better than *Statements after an Arrest under the Immorality Act*, the third play in the South African season, which was written by Athol Fugard alone. I agree with that — I would say that the two collaborative plays are better than anything I've seen that Fugard has done on his own. To say that is not to undervalue Fugard as a playwright, but to give some idea of how good *Sizwe Bansi* and *The Island* are. The season as a whole also showed that Fugard must be a director of genius, for he got performances out of Ben Kingsley and Yvonne Bryceland in *Statements* which rivalled those of Kani and Ntshona in the two collaborative plays.

In an interview, John Kani indicated what may perhaps have been Fugard's single most important influence: 'Athol taught us that we need our art, not propaganda. We tell a story in the simplest form and then we add art to the telling of it. Athol always reminds us that the story is enough and the message will take care of itself. The truth is bigger than ourselves and we should tell it as simply as possible.'

Such an approach can only work when the art brought to the telling of the story is of a very high order, but in these plays it is. There is another point, which can only make British writers envious: the truth being told is so saturated in politics that politics never have to be mentioned.

Julian Mitchell, 'Athol Fugard in London',
African Literature Today, No. 8
(London: Heinemann, 1976), p. 131-2

The Island was *devised*, as opposed to written, by Fugard and the two black actors of the piece, John Kani and Winston Ntshona. *The Island* is indeed an actor's play. It is about acting, it is about acting as a means for the acting of one's life, it is about acting as a form of survival, and it is about acting as a means for *action*. The two men continue to act as humans by using dramatic acting as the means for sustaining their humanity. Improvisation — that tool through which John and Winston understand and practise a role — becomes the means through which John and Winston understand and practise their humanity. Acting, moreover, becomes both shield and sword to the two prisoners: a means for self-protection, for protection of the self, and a means for taking action or acting against their captors, against the state. Fugard thus asserts that acting is no idle art, no end in itself, but the very essence of life and of being human.

Albert Wertheim,
'Political Acting and Political Action: Athol Fugard's *The Island*',
World Literature Written in English, XXVI, No. 2 (1986), p. 245

The Island, the two-character play that Athol Fugard created with the black South African actors John Kani and Winston Ntshona, is one of the more Beckettian works by an author for whom the South African tragedy symbolizes metaphysical struggles that extend far beyond the horrors of apartheid.

Exploring the bond between two cell-mates sentenced for their political activities to hard labour on a remote rocky island, the play suggests that some kind of servitude is an essential condition of life and that a salvation of sorts is to be found only in political and spiritual solidarity with others. As the two cell-mates prepare a two-character presentation of *Antigone* for the annual prison show, they also keep each other's hopes and dreams alive, arguing, remembering, clinging, sharing hopes and fantasies. More than political brothers, in prison they have become collaborators in each other's survival. And when John, the more militant of the pair, is suddenly told that his sentence has been reduced from thirty years to three years, with only three months remaining of his sentence, the reprieve comes as a thunderbolt. How will Winston, the less resilient of the two, survive without him?

The announcement comes as the men are rehearsing *Antigone*, which John has painstakingly taught Winston. In their version, the penultimate dialogue between Creon and Antigone about the individual's duty to the state is to be delivered by Winston wearing crudely improvised prison drag. The farcical costume cloaks a smuggled message of communal resistance and solidarity.

Stephen Holden, *New York Times*,
10 Aug. 1988, p. 17

Dimetos

Two-act play.
Written: on commission, for the Edinburgh Festival.
First public performance: Church Hill Theatre, Edinburgh, 27 Aug. 1975 (dir. Fugard); revised version, Comedy Theatre, London, 24 May 1976 (dir. Fugard; with Paul Scofield as Dimetos, Celia Quicke as Lydia, Yvonne Bryceland as Sophia, and Ben Kingsley as Danilo).
Published: in *Dimetos and Two Early Plays* (1977).

Act One is set in a remote province and Act Two beside the ocean. The action concerns Dimetos, an engineer living in exile on the remote fringes of an empire, recalled to the centre of power by Danilo. Despite the loyal attention of Sophia, his stoic housekeeper, Dimetos has a guilty love for his niece, Lydia. He contrives for Danilo to seduce her, but the girl is so shocked at Dimetos' betrayal that she commits suicide. The second half in a remoter part deals with Dimetos' coming to terms with his loss and acts of penance he must perform; Sophia remains his mainstay, but Lydia recurs to haunt him. He does not return to the known world.

At Edinburgh last year, I had great difficulty in sitting through this piece to the end. The present version, also directed by Fugard (and transferred from Nottingham) at least holds the attention, and not entirely because it stars Paul Scofield. The whole company work to lighten the text, to blow up the gleams of wintry comedy into the occasional flame, and to relieve bleak monotony with emotional contrast. Danilo, the visitor, makes a pass at the girl who rejects him.

That becomes an electrifying episode in the hands of Ben Kingsley and Celia Quicke, who build the scene with such fun and gentleness that its climax comes as a shocking reversal.

Scofield's Dimetos is a remarkable modern addition to his gallery of spiritual recluses and, as usual, he makes the part sound as though it had been written for him. No matter how eloquent a role, he is an actor who always conveys the feeling that the main things have been left unsaid.

Irving Wardle, *The Times*, 25 May 1976, p. 11

It is . . . a fascinating play. Reible has wrought a strongly atmospheric production at the People's Space. There is a heavy, ominous ambience, and there is foreboding in countless passages of dialogue. Marius Weyers as Dimetos gives another magnificent performance. It is strongly controlled playing, building from the relatively placid, withdrawn, ostensibly avuncular figure to the ultimately raging, demented guilt-ridden soul whose scientific knowledge cannot rescue him from his moral dilemma or his mental upset.

Another superb performance comes from Trix Pienaar as Sophia. It is also a strong piece of playing, and she is obviously completely into this role. Aiding her powerful performance is a pulchritudinous strength, and it is difficult to take one's eyes off her when she is on stage.

Mitzi Booysen as Lydia is a credibly trusting, endearing ingenue. Blaise Koch's performance as Danilo is jarring — necessarily so, for he contrasts well with the other three. He is the disturbing catalyst, the dissonant note disturbing the calm. Interestingly, he is the best-spoken part, which again aids the contrast, for the other three sound more distinctly South African.

Not that this is a rigidly South African play — its setting is really universal — but the localized timbre must surely be useful in appreciating the allegory. The dialogue is the key. When Dimetos can speak of the 'challenge of getting a new idea past the barriers of habit and prejudice' and when Danilo can say 'we haven't got the luxury of time any more', you know we are close to home indeed.

Derek Wilson, Argus, Cape Town,
28 Dec. 1981, p. 13

Fugard's thoughts regarding the position and responsibility of an intellectual in society relate to priorities. What is more important: responsibility towards one's neighbour or towards oneself, towards one's work, towards that which one has created? At the end, when his Dimetos, alone on a beach, approaches his fantasies and reflections, Fugard allows his 'deputy' to take on a sort of waiting position. He'd like to hold back 'time', to metamorphose his earlier desires into alternating giving and taking. Here Fugard's piece shifts too much into vague speculation, turns towards philosophical chatter, after having fixed notably exact positions for Dimetos: his flight towards an idyll was, from the very beginning, doomed to impossibility. From his civilized relationships Dimetos brought with him an inability to communicate in his inner emigration. His attempt to build a new, different world foundered on this inability. Those who love him, who stand by him and fight for him, and are ready to suffer for him, are personified in the figure of Sophia. The deleterious effects of his old life continue in the new one. A flight is simply not possible.

Jörn van Dyck, as director of the Kassel premiere, especially brought out these perspectives of the play. His actors succeeded in making solid figures out of Fugard's lyricism and dream-like blurry pictures. In the Kassel Staatstheater the play was given on the stage, and the audience sat behind the stage; the actors worked on a transverse in front of the fire curtain. At the end Dimetos stepped out, beyond the raised fire curtain, into a empty auditorium. There, where otherwise the audience would be seated, Dimetos, alone, crouched and philosophized. It was a nice, geodramaturgically thought-illuminating touch that said more than suggested by Fugard's text. This theatricality triumphed over the all-too-troubled meditations of the author. It was a very successful production.

Gerhard Rohde,
Frankfurter Algemeine Zeitung, 5 June 1982, p. 18
(translated by Barbara Perlmutter)

A Lesson from Aloes

Full-length play.
Written: from the early 1960s, during which it is set.

First production: Market Theatre, Johannesburg, 30 Nov. 1978
(dir. Fugard; with Marius Weyers as Piet, Shelagh Holliday as
Gladys, and Bill Curry as Steve).

First American production: Yale Repertory Theatre, New Haven,
28 March 1980 (dir. Fugard; with Harris Yulin, Maria Tucci, and
James Earl Jones); trans. Playhouse, Broadway, 17 Nov. 1980.

First London production: Cottesloe Theatre, 10 July 1980 (dir. Fugard;
with the original cast). During the British run, BBC-TV showed a
documentary made by Ross Devenish in Johannesburg of the
rehearsals and early performances of the first production.

Published: Oxford University Press, 1981.

The play is set in the backyard of the Afrikaner Piet Bezuidenhout's suburban house in Algoa Park, Port Elizabeth — an outdoor dining area and garden surrounded by aloes in pots, and also including the bedroom area, the domain of Gladys, his wife. She is preparing for Steve Daniels and family to arrive for a last supper prior to their departure into exile — Steve has recently been released from imprisonment for political crimes. Their marriage is haunted by three traumatic past events: Piet's activism with Steve, which may involve his betrayal of his friend; a security police search which has led to the confiscation of Gladys's most private diaries; and the resultant state of Gladys, who teeters on the edge of another crack-up. Steve arrives alone and cannot stay, so that the second half involves the dismantling of all the preparations. Steve still suspects Piet, but cuts his losses and leaves. Gladys now suspects Piet, and this drives her over the edge. Piet is left to endure, and we are sure of his innocence.

Sometimes a new play comes along that makes all others look like toys for children. And it turns the whole odd business of theatre, and acting and dressing-up, into something that is actually worth the serious attention of adults.

Athol Fugard's *A Lesson from Aloes* at the Cottesloe is not there for fun. It has work to do. In doing it, it provides a turbulent emotional experience and a new insight into the effects of hatred, stupidity, and fear.

John Barber, *Daily Telegraph*,
11 July 1980, p. 9

A Lesson from Aloes

With only three characters, here is the dramatic equivalent, not of a novel, but of a poetically allusive short story by some such master as Lawrence or Patrick White. Marius Weyers is nothing short of superb as an Afrikaner misfit who, in his stubborn determination to fulfil himself in soil however barren, so much resembles the aloes that he cultivates; and Shelagh Holliday gives a haunting performance as his wife, fluttering like some wounded bird between one nervous breakdown and another. There is nothing more moving to be seen in London at present.

Francis King, *Sunday Telegraph*,
13 July 1980, p. 16

It takes a lot to get an inner suburbanite to trek out of the city for theatrical experiences, but *A Lesson from Aloes* more than justifies the trip to Monash. The play, the latest by South African playwright Athol Fugard, won the New York Drama Critics' Circle Award as the best play of the 1980-81 season on Broadway, and it's easy to see why.

Ostensibly a conventional drama — in that it depends for its effect on the audience being deeply involved rather than alienated observers — it works as a mystery (who dobbed Steve in to the security police?) and as a psychological drama which builds sustained tension from our inability to foresee what will happen next.

It is one of a few of Fugard's plays to be specifically set in time (1963), but it gradually becomes clear that this date signals the passing of the time when people of different races in South Africa could work together in mass organizations, and those who wanted to oppose the regime were deprived of any activity other than violent terrorism or passive submission.

Piet, a humane but naive Afrikaner, chooses to wait out apartheid; his Anglo-Saxon wife Gladys teeters on the brink of insanity; and his ex-comrade, the coloured worker Steve, leaves the country on a one-way exit permit rather than submit to the endless frustrations of the regime. Not much choice for them ... even less for black South Africans.

The characters are clearly separated by accent, language and the experiences they have undergone — symbols of a society morally and politically structured on race. The set, at first sight elaborate for a Fugard play, becomes only another kind of Group Area, a ghetto for whites as barren as Boesman and Lena's rubbish tip.

The production by Gillian Owen is intelligent and tight, making the most of the nuances of domestic routine and the few crises caused by the intrusion of police into private lives.

But the greatest delight offered by this sombre and disturbing play comes from the acting performances — Anthony Wheeler's unshakable confidence as Piet, the Gladys of Olive Bodill, an actress who can invest the smallest gesture with meaning, and Phillip Hinton's subtly physical characterization of Steve.

Margaret Munro, *Melbourne Times*, 1 July 1981, p. 7

The Drummer

Playlet for improvisation.
Written: on commission, for the Annual Festival of New American Plays at the Actors Theatre, Louisville, Kentucky.
First production: March 1980.
Published: in *Selected Shorter Plays* (1990).

All of [the] small-arms fire in 'The America Project' comes from foreign writers and, over all, their targets seem too easy and their attitude isn't exactly dripping with generosity. The best of them, South Africa's Athol Fugard, makes the deftest contribution in The Drummer, *in which Dierk Toporzysek, combining the techniques of Red Skelton, Jackie Gleason, and Marcel Marceau, plays a tattered bum playing a crazy percussion concert on a trash can in a New York alley.*

Jack Kroll, *Newsweek*, 31 March 1980, p. 70

'Master Harold' . . . and the Boys

Full-length play, based on an autobiographical episode.
First production: Yale Repertory Theatre, 12 March 1982 (dir. Fugard; with Zakes Mokae as Sam and Danny Glover as Willie); trans. Broadway, 4 May.
First South African production: Market Theatre, Johannesburg, 22 March 1983 (dir. Fugard; with John Kani as Sam, Ramolao Makhene as Willy, and Duart Sylwain as Hally).
First London production: Market Theatre production, Cottesloe Theatre, 25 Nov. 1983 (dir. Fugard).
Published: New York: Knopf, 1982; Oxford University Press, 1983; New York: Penguin: 1984; in *Selected Plays* (1987).

The Saint George's Park Tea Room in Port Elizabeth in the 1940s on a desultory and windy afternoon that will produce no

'Master Harold' ... and the Boys

customers. Sam the head waiter and Willie the kitchen-help are variously cleaning and tidying, while the real 'boy' of the piece, 'Master' Harold, has school homework to do. Offstage, mother is with father, who is hospitalized. The action involves discussion of real educational issues, contrasting Hally's bumptious book-learning with Sam's practising for the ballroom dancing championships. Let down by his real father, Hally insults Sam, spitting in his face, to which Sam responds by lowering his pants. Hally storms off, leaving the two black brothers to dance to the jukebox and close up.

It's the first of my plays that has ever been done for the first time outside of South Africa. I've always had a sense that the plays that lie behind me — *Aloes*, *Boesman*, and the others . . . that South Africa was a half-owner of the rights. This one belongs to me; this one's mine.

Athol Fugard, Yale Reports, 1981-82 Season

The three characters in this sublime memory play are marked by their youthful ardour, and the appropriate central metaphor is ballroom dancing. This is an Astaire-ized vision of a ballroom where dancers smoothly glide, an ideal world 'in which accidents don't happen . . . a world without collisions'.

The playwright is speaking, first of all, about the bond between a lonely white teenage boy and an adult black man who becomes his best friend and surrogate father. The youngster is the master, the man is the servant. But which one is really the teacher? In the course of a rainy, revelatory afternoon, the man — one of two waiters in a tearoom run by the boy's mother — instructs the teenager in the 'steps' of life, a lesson that echoes far beyond the café-classroom. He offers him a curriculum in the meaning of compassion, and the boy, who may or may not understand the message, is, we surmise, an awakening artist as well as prodigal son.

Mel Gussow, New York Times, 21 March 1982, p. 4

How biographical is the play? The dedication reads, 'For Sam and H. D. F.'. Sam was a real person, a black man, whom Fugard valued in his youth. 'H. D. F.' are the initials of Mr. Fugard's father, who loved to play jazz piano in a combo and died twenty years ago. In a sense, *'Master Harold'* looks at two father figures, although Mr. Fugard cautions against exact parallels. 'Of course the elements relate to my childhood', he said. 'But I've taken poetic licence, as Hally says. If the play is valid it is as a piece of theatre, not a personal history.'

Now in his late forties, with a lively beard that gives him the appearance of a diminutive Shaw, Mr. Fugard alternates between reticence and flashes of fire, rapping a listener on the knee for emphasis, cocking his head to absorb the questions.

How long did it take to write *'Master Harold'*? 'For years I tried to come up with a play about just Sam and Willie', he said. 'Then, eighteen months ago, I added this little white boy ... and the kinetic energy that that released was amazing.' When Hally explodes at his two friends, in a nightmare vision of life as a cripples' dance ('broken spiders trying to do the quick step'), it's as if the despotism bottled up inside him had burst out.

'That speech was the hardest thing in the play', said Mr. Fugard. 'It was so close to my own feelings of long ago — and I had to do it *dramatically*.' The script expanded from 20 to 65 pages, and now runs 105 minutes without intermission. 'So you could really say the play's been gestating since I was fifteen years old ... since those rainy days thirty-five years ago, when they'd dance and I'd stomp around like a little Hitler.'

How did *'Master Harold'* come to Yale? 'Indirectly, thanks to James Earl Jones', Mr. Fugard said. 'Because he'd gotten hold of a copy of *Aloes*, and showed it to Lloyd Richards, saying he'd love to be in it. So we did that one, and they did *Boesman* next season. It was a very congenial atmosphere, so I offered them *'Master Harold'*.' In fact, this marks the first time a Fugard play has received its premiere outside his homeland. 'All the others belonged partly to South Africa, in a strange way', he mused. 'But this one — this one's mine.'

Did Fugard the director harmonize with Fugard the playwright? 'Put it this way', he said, laughing. 'Never again will I write a play with twelve chairs on the set. Talk about a staging challenge! But I do seem to shift hats pretty well.' He also directed *Aloes* at Yale and on Broadway and *Sizwe Bansi* and *The Island* in New York. A frequent actor as well, Mr. Fugard admires performers' efforts to probe the text, to make it live on a stage. One stage direction has Hally 'trying to look like Tolstoy' ('We had some laughs trying to work that one out'), and one of the play's emotional peaks — Hally spitting in Sam's face — required many sessions before the right nuance and timing were achieved....

Does it make him nervous to be labelled a South African writer? 'Not if you mean in the sense Bill Faulkner was a "Southern writer",' he said. 'He's the man who gave me confidence to stick it out, to stay in one place. To me, the curse of the theatre today is generalizing. You need a place, you need the reality *first*.'

'Master Harold' ... and the Boys

'Master Harold' is a departure from recent Fugard works in its abundance of humour. 'I wanted to have fun this time, especially after a dour play like *Aloes*', he said. 'At first it was tough, recovering the light touch, but all through rehearsals I kept telling the actors, 'Think levity, *then* gravity".'

Doesn't the tea-room setting of *'Master Harold'* with its jukebox represent a change for Mr. Fugard? Like the setting of *A Lesson from Aloes*, it is a middle-class environment, far from the black shantytowns and desolate landscapes of earlier plays. 'You're right, though I'd substitute "personal" for "middle-class",' the playwright said. 'I started out with characters who *had* less. But you go through changes, and why should every play lead organically to the next? You have to turn the corner, take a detour. Like my favourite Russian proverb, "To live a life is not to cross a field".'

Steve Lawson, 'Fugard Tries a Lighter Touch',
New York Times, 2 May 1982, p. 27

Johannesburg, 23 March. — *'Master Harold'* ... *and the Boys*, Athol Fugard's confessional drama about a white adolescent's initiation in the uses of racial power, has come home to South Africa, and it left its multiracial audience at the opening night performance here on Tuesday visibly shaken.

When the lights dimmed on the powerful last scene, in which the two black waiters affirm their self-respect in the embrace of a slow, heart-rending fox trot, roughly half the audience rose to give the play's three actors a standing ovation. The rest had yet to emerge from a private world of grief and loss into which the play had seemingly plunged them. Many, blacks and whites, were crying.

The play, easily the most accessible to foreign audiences that Mr. Fugard has written, had a comparable impact on Broadway, where it recently completed a ten-month run. But there was a palpable difference in the way it was experienced here, for its broad themes about a flight from friendship and a wilful failure of understanding did not have to be reinterpreted in universal terms. They were painfully specific to South Africa and the lives of the people the play moved Tuesday night.

Joseph Lelyveld, *New York Times*, 24 Mar. 1983, p. 16

As I've known the man and I've worked with the man for quite some time, I think it is an important milestone in his life, to decide to use a true incident in his life in the attempt to bridge the widening gap between the peoples of my country, in the attempt to say something in a country where silence is the norm. It's again an attempt to improve the relationships between black and white because the entire South African white society has a Sam, a servant in their lives, and these are the things that they would not consider even when they try in their political sense to improve the relationship. They would change certain laws, relax certain things, but they will never touch the attitude, and I feel this play deals with the attitudes.

Sam is a great fighter for decency in the world. That's how it does it for me, just decency, a decent relationship between two people, a decent relationship between people of the world. Humanity, just being a man. That's what I teach the boy all my life, to be a man, a human being, which in the end, of course, reminds me I'm a boy.

John Kani, *BBC Arts and Africa*, 25 Dec. 1983

The Road to Mecca

A play in two acts, suggested by the life and work of Helen Martins of New Bethesda.
First production: Yale Repertory Theatre, 1 May 1984 (dir. Fugard; with Carmen Mathews as Miss Helen, Marianne Owen as Elsa, and Tom Aldredge as Marius).
First South African production: Market Theatre, Johannesburg, 27 Nov. 1984 (dir. Fugard; with Yvonne Bryceland as Miss Helen, Elize Cawood as Elsa, and Louis van Niekerk as Marius).
First London production: Lyttelton Theatre, 22 Feb. 1985 (dir. Fugard; with Yvonne Bryceland, Charlotte Cornwell, and Bob Peck).
First Broadway production: Promenade Theatre, 1 May 1988 (dir. Fugard; with Yvonne Bryceland, Amy Irving, and himself).
Published: London; Boston: Faber and Faber, 1985.

Set in Helen Martins's living space in the desolate Karoo town of New Bethesda — an extraordinary bungalow interior transformed by her skylights, glowing mosaics, and unique sculptures. The time is autumn, 1974 — literally the autumn of her life. Shunned by the small community as an eccentric, she has only two visitors: Elsa, her young liberal soul-mate who looks after her whenever she can get away from Cape Town, and the local dominee, Marius Byleveld, who has found Miss Helen a room in an old-age retreat. Elsa also suspects that Miss Helen can no longer cope. In effect, they both fight for the old woman's soul. Miss Helen resists both of them, forced in the end to reveal her quirky vision — filling the stage with candlelight and her glowing faith in her 'Mecca'. This postpones her departure, Marius is defeated, and the two women celebrate.

The setting and lighting design effectively create Helen's multi-coloured home which transforms itself after the setting of the Karoo sun into a temple of light and sparkle. The enormous sculptures visible in Helen's yard — one with head uplifted and arms outstretched — are particularly expressive of Helen's own vision and quest for freedom. Late in the play, Elsa asks Helen why she never sculpted an angel. Helen replies that if she had, her angel would not be pointing towards Heaven, but would point towards the East — towards Mecca and freedom — and would, therefore, 'divert all those Christian souls' passing by from their inflexible Calvinist beliefs.

Jerry Dickey, Theatre Journal,
XXXVI, No. 4 (Dec. 1984), p. 527

Since 1975 and the production of *Dimetos* (his least successful play) Fugard has turned away from the immediate social and political realities of South Africa, exploring instead the psychology of the isolated white consciousness — most persuasively, perhaps, in the guilt-ridden self-portrait of *'Master Harold' . . . and the Boys*. *The Road to Mecca* continues this trend. Unlike Dimetos, Miss Helen is granted transcendence; but is she the only person who is to be so liberated?

Dennis Walder, Times Literary Supplement,
15 March 1985, p. 289

One explanation for the audience appeal of *Mecca* at the eleventh Spoleto Festival, USA, is the long-awaited chance for Americans to see Bryceland and Fugard perform together — a first in this country. And there is a drama behind this good fortune.

Though Fugard and Bryceland had talked about her performing the central, pivotal character of Helen Martins, a seventy-year-old reclusive sculptress, before *Mecca*'s world premiere at the Yale Repertory Theatre in May 1984, Bryceland did not appear in that production because American Actors' Equity insisted that Fugard use an all-American cast. Thereafter, Fugard refused to have a New York production *without* Bryceland as Miss Helen. Again, Actors' Equity denied Bryceland permission to perform in New York on the grounds that to do so would deprive an American actress of a major role and, moreover, that Bryceland was not 'an international star'.

The stand-off between Fugard and Actors' Equity led to his staging *Mecca* first at the Market Theatre in Johannesburg and then at the National Theatre in London, where it was so successful that it ran for two seasons and enabled Bryceland to win the coveted Olivier Award for best actress. With the impasse between Fugard and Actors' Equity worked out, Spoleto's audiences will have a chance to see not one, but two London-based actress-protagonists (Bryceland and Cornwell), as well as Fugard himself as their antagonist.

Nancy Kearns, *Creative Loafing*, Charleston, 23 May 1987, p. 1

The artist at the centre of Athol Fugard's new play, *The Road to Mecca*, does not want to change the world. Miss Helen, as she is known, is a reclusive old widow in a dusty, isolated village in the South African wilderness. Her art is an oddball collection of concrete sculptures exhibited in her garden — wise men, mermaids, and animals that she calls her 'Mecca'. Her sparse audience is her neighbours, most of whom regard her not as an artist but as the town madwoman, a laughing stock.

Since Mr. Fugard is an artist who does want to change the world — and arguably has — one might wonder why he is telling us the story of Miss Helen. The author of such indelible tragedies of apartheid as *Blood Knot* and *'Master Harold' . . . and the Boys* would seem to have scant connection with an eccentric whose art is obsessively, idiosyncratically private and devoid of political content. But the connection is made, and, once it is, the play at the Promenade becomes a career summation, its author's own 'Mecca'. The stage is flooded with light — literally and figuratively — as Mr. Fugard finds in Miss Helen's artistic credo a cathartic statement of what it means to be a true artist in any place, at any time.

The revelation is overwhelming. In a living room glittering in candlelight, Yvonne Bryceland, as Miss Helen, is trying to explain her mission to Mr. Fugard, who plays the role of Marius, the village's hidebound minister. With her matted silver hair, sandals, and bulky clothing, Ms. Bryceland looks almost like a bag lady. Mr. Fugard, dark and stern, is a narrow puritan who would like to usher his rebellious old friend into the Sunshine Home for the Aged. But when Miss Bryceland, her eyes blazing and her voice rising, waves her fists in exaltation to describe her initial vision of her 'Mecca' as 'a city of light and colour more splendid than anything I ever imagined', she forces us and Marius to see that wondrous spectacle too. And as she recounts what it took to realize that vision — the hard work of grinding beer bottles and mixing cement with her arthritic hands, the courage to survive the ostracism of her community — we see even more about the will that drove her on.

Frank Rich, *New York Times*, 13 Apr. 1988, p. 14

Athol Fugard's base language is standard South African English, but his linguistic environments vary greatly, including the polyglot townships (*The Blood Knot, Sizwe Bansi Is Dead*), urban Afrikaans (*Hello and Goodbye*) and 'Kaaps' (*Boesman and Lena*), urban English (*'Master Harold' . . . and the Boys*) and rural Afrikaans (*The Road to Mecca*). Clearly language differences, language variants, and the use of the transliteration process are basic to Fugard's dialogue, and to his dramaturgy — an issue which has had a significant impact on later South African writing. Each writer has inevitably always written only in one language — either Afrikaans (P. G. du Plessis, Chris Barnard), Afrikaans *or* English (Adam Small), or English (Stephen Black, Fugard, Paul Slabolepszy), despite the fact that they were writing about polyglot communities and basically within the realist tradition. Viewed historically, the convention employed by these writers is inevitable, since, besides their own socio-cultural identity and linguistic bent, a number of external influences — some fundamental, some circumstantial — dictated its use.

> Temple Hauptfleisch, 'Citytalk, Theatretalk:
> Dialect, Dialogue, and Multilingual Theatre in South Africa',
> *English in Africa*, Grahamstown, XVI, No. 1 (May 1990), p. 80

A Place with the Pigs

Full-length play in four scenes.
Written: as a 'personal parable', provoked by the true story of Pavel Navrotsky, a deserter from the Soviet army in the Second World War, who spent forty-one years in hiding in his own pigsty.
First production: Yale Repertory Theatre, 24 March 1987 (dir. Fugard; with himself as Pavel and Suzanne Shepherd as Praskovya).
First South African production: Market Theatre production at Rhodes Theatre, Grahamstown, 9 July 1987 (dir. Fugard; with himself as Pavel and Linda Meiring).
First London production: Cottesloe Theatre, 16 Feb. 1988 (dir. Fugard; with Jim Broadbent and Linda Basset).
Published: London; Boston: Faber and Faber, 1988.

Set in the pigsty within the barn of Pavel Navrotsky, the deserter from the Russian army, where he has been in hiding for four decades and become near-deranged, sustained by his long-suffering 'widow', Praskovya. A black comedy about the fears governing Pavel, this play involves two main episodes — his preparations to give himself up, and then his disguised outing to the village one night, enjoying his first taste of freedom. In the end he learns that to free himself he must free the pigs as well, and the play concludes with the shut-in set opening out, and humans and beasts charging forth to a new day.

A Place with the Pigs, now enjoying its world premiere engagement at the Yale Repertory Theatre, is a surprise: an Athol Fugard play *not* set in South Africa. The play takes place instead, as its title indicates, with the pigs — or, as the programme says, in 'a pigsty, in a small village, somewhere in the author's imagination'. That's fine, but doesn't every play unfold somewhere in its author's imagination? When a writer must inform an audience of that fact, one immediately starts worrying that the piece at hand is not fully imagined.

The fears are justified with *A Place with the Pigs*, at least at this stage of its development.

Frank Rich, *New York Times*, 3 Apr. 1987, p. 14

Why does one have to work hard with some very obvious — and often trite — images? I hope this is not a case of the Emperor's new clothes. And speaking of clothes, at least you get to see Fugard in drag.

Ketan Lakhani, *Cue*, Grahamstown, 10 July 1987

Fugard creates his own terms and it would be small-minded and self-defeating not to see the play in those terms. *A Place with the Pigs* significantly extends our notions of the theatrically possible. It pioneers.

Robert Greig, *Cue*, Grahamstown, 10 July 1987

Something has shifted in his work and in the concerns underlying his work. Where plays like *The Blood Knot* or *Hello and Goodbye* dealt with conditions which were imposed by outside forces, in recent years Fugard's work has been moving towards meditations on freedom and the uses and abuses of that freedom.

But not, he insists, at the expense of any 'political' content. Current definitions of politics, he says as the lightning cracks about him, and flame pours from his eyes, are so stupid, so pathetically limited and limiting. Freedom then is a political thing.

Ivor Powell, *Weekly Mail*, Johannesburg, 14 Aug. 1987, p. 22

A Place with the Pigs

About three years ago Fugard forced himself into change, cutting out booze, giving up smoking, and expanding his consciousness. 'I started to clean up my life. There is a revolution taking place in South Africa and there is a revolution in my private life. It sounds like being born again but I must mention the birth of a new Fugard, or something akin to that.

'For better or worse my life is in tandem with South African society. But I don't want that to sound like a fait accompli. There are changes in the molecular structure that are spreading in all directions all the time.'

It was a small news item in the *New York Times* that inspired the latest play, *A Place with the Pigs*. The mention of a Russian soldier who deserted his army and spent the next forty-one years of his life hiding in a pigsty prompted deep research into what a man can and can't live without.

Fugard is aware of his age and is taking advantage of it. 'At this stage of my life I am concerned with two things. One, by the time you get to fifty-five you're getting into a situation of diminishing energies and I must harness, look after, and husband what energy there is. Two, there is a new sense of adventure in my medium. *Pigs* is a departure, a new direction. I am discovering how marvellously free the theatre is, as opposed to film.'

If Fugard's career is indeed a parallel with the emergence of the new South Africa, then there is hope. For all the seriousness and wisdom brooding beneath those bushy eyebrows, his approach to the future is joyous, almost mischievous. Both he and his country know what they want and where they are going.

John Michell, 'Odyssey of a Loner', The Star, Johannesburg, 9 Aug. 1987, p. 11

Somewhere in the action of *A Place with the Pigs* (Market Theatre, Johannesburg), the central character, Pavel, starts to laugh, stops suddenly, and says to himself in sheer astonishment, 'I am actually laughing again.' I felt exactly the same way as I watched this fascinating play because over the years Fugard has never given me much to laugh about. Yet there I was, laughing from the belly at hilarious lines which are genuinely and organically part of his serious dramatic intention. . . .

He shows us a man cut off from the world, making his own laws, rules, and morality but living in squalid fear. He talks a lot about changing things but never does, and in his isolation he becomes cruel, vicious, and less than human, all because he is too afraid to go outside and face the comrades. Sound familiar?

Of course it does, but it is pleasing to see that Fugard does not make this the whole and explicit point of the play. He allows some room for the art of evocative drama alongside his customary Significant Statements, and by doing so he produces his best play in years.

Barry Ronge, Sunday Times, Johannesburg,
23 Aug. 1987, p. 20

Fugard, I think, should have remained silent. Instead *A Place with the Pigs* reveals, sadly, the consequences of the playwright's own voluntary removal of himself from the social life of this country. By analogy (a Russian military deserter lives for forty years in a pigsty), the play introduces questions of dignity and freedom. . . . We have, after all, been trained to define 'good art' as oblique, complex, nuanced, subtle, universal. Fugard's avoidance, at this particular time, of our own extremely narrow tolerances of dignity and freedom is disappointing. His 'universalism' seems a luxury.

Michael Chapman,
'The Liberated Zone: the Possibilities of Imaginative
Expression in a State of Emergency', English Academy Review,
Johannesburg, V (1988), p. 34-5

My Children! My Africa!

Full-length play in two acts, and eleven scenes.
First production: Market Theatre, 27 June 1989 (dir. Fugard; with John Kani as Mr. M., Kathy-Jo Ross as Isabel, and Rapulana Seiphemo as Thami, and with ushers of the theatre as the children of Zolile High School).
First New York production: Perry Street Theatre, 18 Dec. 1989 (dir. Fugard; with John Kani, Lisa Fugard, and Courtney B. Vance).
First London production: Cottesloe Theatre, 28 Aug. 1990 (dir. Fugard; with John Kani, Lisa Fugard, and Rapulana Seiphemo).
Published: London: Faber and Faber, 1990; in *My Children! My Africa! and Selected Shorter Plays* (1990).

Set mainly in the classroom of Zolile High School, Camdeboo, in the Karoo, 1984, though the forestage represents various meeting places. Mr. M. is refereeing a debate about rights in South Africa between his favourite pupil, Thami, and the chief spokesperson of the visiting white school, Isabel. The debate is to be extended with the two as a team in a forthcoming literary

My Children! My Africa!

quiz, the rehearsals for which bring the two pupils close. The boycott of 'black education' intervenes, and Thami the activist is set against Mr. M., who betrays the ringleaders. Thami offers his teacher the chance to escape, but Mr. M. obdurately insists on preaching his message of collaboration; he is necklaced by the crowd. Thami goes into exile and bids Isabel farewell. She is left to pronounce Mr. M's epitaph.

In debating the values of a humanist education in a context of radical political action, all three characters become glued to a web, in which a movement from any one of them tears the emotional fabric of the others. They are inextricably caught, bruised, damaged, and deformed by the personal and political identities determined for them by their context.

That context — Fugard's Africa — and these people — Fugard's children — are subjected in this play to analysis by a politically more probing Fugard than we have previously seen. One suspects that Fugard has moved around on this web in a way which has been equally painful for him.

For all three characters, and for the playwright, words are not means but ends. In them resides the substance of relationships, the articulation of identity, and for Fugard the very form of the play. Here words are not merely a method but a dramatic experience. Speech, in this play, is action. Fugard does not clutter his stage with mere activity as a background to dialogue. The characters engage the audience as antagonists in the drama.

There are few moments in any staged drama to compare with Kani's gloriously realized statue of justice caught momentarily spellbound by the sight of a book in one hand and a stone in the other. Nor can one deny the articulate common sense of Fugard's conception of the staging of the play, brilliantly reinforced by some of the most intelligent stage lighting to be seen in . . . Johannesburg, with Mannie Manim breaking new ground with colour and intensity as characters in the drama.

John Kani's performance is the finest imaginable. He wears this character like an old habit invested with new energy. He plays the schoolteacher in a minor key, as if from a vale of tears, at one moment, and reaches resonant oratorical heights at the next. Kani the actor is Myalatya the teacher, and they are both raconteurs who know their audiences intimately. Fugard's play fits this actor like a glove, and he knows exactly when to raise the clenched fist at his audience, and when to extend the welcoming hand. And how to seduce them.

It has been fashionable in recent years to distinguish between cultural work which domesticates (showing how people should cope with things as they are) and cultural work which liberates (showing people how things can and should be changed). Much of Fugard's previous work has been (somewhat unfairly) pigeonholed in the former category. With this play he takes his audience forcefully into a symbolic debate which is not merely liberal but liberating.

Ian Steadman, *Weekly Mail*, Johannesburg,
30 June 1989, p. 21-2

The subject of *My Children! My Africa!* is situated differently from that of *A Place with the Pigs*. Instead of middle-aged angst, which Fugard may have a right to, but which during a vicious, day-after-day state of emergency seems to have marginal importance, this time his subject is squarely in the arena of the main action in the South Africa of the recent past (1984): the schoolroom. No one can fail to recognize that blackboard and chalk, the school-bell and register — the only props used.

Two of the three characters in *My Children! My Africa!* are indeed 'children' — at least, the right-less youths of South Africa. There they are in their pre-matriculation uniforms that subtly over the years have come not to mean promise and fulfilment, but oppression and regimentation: bitter obedience to an untenable moral order and its deforming brainwash.

Just as the country chafes for freedom, so do Thami and Isabel: their aching, battling decencies struggle, practically throttle, on the indecencies of a system so dishonest and death-dispensing that we root for them and their future from the start. By the end — for this is the story of their bleeding, devastating friendship and how it is all but destroyed — one can only gaspingly applaud their endurance. May the rising generation be just as resilient. May the future be *theirs*.

Stephen Gray, *New Theatre Quarterly*, VI, No. 21 (Feb. 1990), p. 26

I wouldn't like to flatter myself by calling it a progression or development, but I know there is a difference between the florid, juicy kind of writing in *The Blood Knot* and the much drier style I have now. In an overall sense I would like to believe there has been a refining process at work. I don't slap as many colours on the canvas.

But also in terms of what one might call the 'spirit' of the work, I think it is a matter of turning more inward, leaving — not completely abandoning — the social context of my characters. Except that then, suddenly, there's a thing called *My Children! My Africa!* which confounded me.

The adventure with that play owes a lot to an evening in London at a production of *Antony and Cleopatra*. The programme included a paragraph by Granville Barker about how total Shakespeare's command over the stage was, and how he could just move the action both externally and inwardly, any way he wanted.

And I suddenly thought, my God, wouldn't it be marvellous to reclaim the stage with that sort of freedom, you don't even have to tell anybody where you are, you just bring out two characters.

That was how I tried to put it down on paper. And it was such an adventure when the challenge came of staging it, to match the freedom with which I had first written the words.

Fugard, interviewed by André Brink,
Leadership, Cape Town, 13 March 1990, p. 76

b: Television Plays

The Occupation

A camera script.
Unperformed.
Published: *Contrast*, Cape Town, Apr. 1964; in *Ten One-Act Plays*, ed. Cosmo Pieterse (London: Heinemann Educational, 1968); *Selected Shorter Plays* (1990).

A sherry-gang of white drop-outs move in on and occupy a once-grand mansion, now deserted, in a Karoo landscape. Serge and Cappie relive their past, retaining the ranks they held as South African soldiers in the invasion of Italy during the Second World War. Barend, an independent tramp, fights for dominance over them and possessively takes the only bed. The others camp about a fire made on the floor of the living-room, initiating the new recruit, Koosie, into the techniques of begging and being a hobo. By dawn they are ready to move on.

Mille Miglia

A play for television.
Written: while his passport was removed, for BBC-2's Theatre 625, on the 'factual' British victory at the Italian Grand Prix in 1955.

First production: 5 Aug. 1968 (dir. Robin Midgley; with Michael Bryant as Stirling Moss and Ronald Lacey as Denis Jenkinson).
Stage adaptation: by David Muir, as *Drivers*, Outer Space, Cape Town, 18 July 1973 (dir. David Muir; with Bill Curry and Bill Flynn).
Published: in *Selected Shorter Plays* (1990).

The preparations for the race, featuring the unique partnership of Moss and Jenkinson, whom we know are destined to win. The settings are the various interiors of Italy — garages, cafés, hotel rooms. The play closes in on the bond of dependence between the two, forged while devising a route-map and a code of hand-signals to be used accurately at speed. The two keyed-up participants explode into doubts and nervousness and suspicion, but edgily regain a link of trust through rehearsing the race on chairs. The action ends as they go down to the start.

Because of the very nature of the play (small cast), and because of the limits within which Fugard has had to work (studio interiors only), *Mille Miglia* shows nothing of the famous race itself. The play ends almost as it started, the two men sitting together, but this time on the starting line in their car. This is the climax up to which *Mille Miglia* has been building. The race itself is of little significance.

For, as Fugard says, this is not a play about motor racing. It is about two men waiting . . . waiting for that moment in time when the game becomes life.

Peter Mason, *Sunday Tribune*, Durban, 21 Jan. 1968

---

c: Feature Films

Boesman and Lena

Adaptation by Fugard of his own stage play.
Written: 1971-73, and filmed on location around Port Elizabeth, 1973.
Released: 1974 (a Bluewater production, dir. Ross Devenish; with Fugard and Yvonne Bryceland).

Boesman and Lena *works far better as a film than it ever did as a play .... In the film, the pre-title sequence of the destruction of the shanty town — in which the characters are virtually bulldozed out of their existence — provides a strong visual motivation for the later development and a facet of Boesman's personality, only suggested in the play by Lena's playful mimicry of it, is forcibly depicted.*

Depicted, and at the same time given a new dimension. In the play, Lena taunts Boesman with his servility in the presence of the white man. We immediately relate this to the traditional about-face of the bully when confronted with authority. In the film, we see Boesman seeming to toady to the demolishers, but we are not deceived. What he is doing is clearly a savage parody of the white man's concept of the coloured. When the foreman smiles approvingly at his assistant, 'They don't make them like that anymore', we cut to a close-up of Boesman's face, his screwed-up eyes generating hate. ...

It is a film every South African should see.

Raeford Daniel, *Rand Daily Mail*, Johannesburg,
22 Nov. 1973, p. 7

The Guest

Original screenplay, based on an episode in the life of Eugène Marais, from the biography by Leon Rousseau, and filmed on location in the Transvaal, 1976.

Written: in collaboration with Ross Devenish. Original title: *The Guest at Steenkampskraal.*

Premiered: on BBC-2 TV, as a 'Film International', 5 March 1977 (a Guest production, dir. Ross Devenish; with Fugard, Marius Weyers, and Wilma Stockenström).

Published: Johannesburg: Donker, 1977.

Set on a farm near Heidelberg in the Transvaal highveld, in winter landscape. In 1926 Eugène N. Marais (1871-1936), the Afrikaans poet and naturalist, author of The Soul of the Ape, *arrives there with his stern friend, the doctor A. G. Visser, as a paying guest, ostensibly to complete his nature studies in seclusion, but also to recover from his morphine addiction. The sympathetic farming family endure his agonizing withdrawal, during which he befriends their youngest child as a soul-mate. His rapport with baboons and the surroundings is explored, as well as his dark lyricism. Unable to dry out, he bribes a labourer to smuggle him doses, and he leaves the farm with a curse on his lips — some of his most troubling poems.*

Steenkampskraal, the farm to which Marais had gone in 1926 in order to reduce his morphine dependence, provided what we were looking for. The film would begin with Marais' arrival at the farm and would end when he finally leaves several months later. This small episode contains the elements of Marais' total story; besides, the period at Steenkampskraal was repeated again and again in Marais' life. He was always the guest 'in someone else's home'. A not unimportant advantage of this locale was that it provided us with perhaps a more ambitious film but also, ironically, a less expensive one.

Ross Devenish, *Star*, Johannesburg, 10 Sept. 1977, p. 3

Marigolds in August

Original screenplay.
Written: in collaboration with Ross Devenish, based on earlier notes by Fugard, and filmed on location in and around Port Elizabeth, 1979.
Premiered: at the Johannesburg Film Festival, 21 Apr. 1980 (a Serpent Southern production, dir. Ross Devenish; with John Kani, Winston Ntshona, and Fugard).
Published: Johannesburg: Donker, 1982.

Three Port Elizabeth characters interact in a day of minor incidents: crippled Daan the odd-job man and gardener, Melton the work-seeker, and Paulus the snake-catcher. The title refers to premature hopes: marigolds planted in August wither before the African spring in September.

The latest collaboration between Athol Fugard, the writer, and Ross Devenish, the director, is a simple, clean, and moving statement about the painful dilemmas of poverty under the limitations imposed by South Africa's racial laws. Two principle issues are illuminated. The first is

Feature Films

that the need to hold on to what employment there is can make a gentle man use cold, angry suspicion as a barrier to natural sympathy. The second is that burglary is a lesser sin than to return to a starving family with empty hands.

Rina Minervini, *Rand Daily Mail*, Johannesburg,
24 April 1980, p. 12

We shot the film on the actual locations where those characters lived and where the incidents took place. Paulus used to come out of the bush and walk past my garden and I'd greet him and ask how things had gone and he'd empty his bag of snakes on my lawn and show me what his day's catch was. We wanted, Ross Devenish the director and myself, to tell a story of people like that, using a medium that so grossly ignores them in terms of the South African context — to tell a story of relevance and significance for a black audience.

Fugard, *BBC Arts and Africa*, 10 July 1980

While this conflict has its own absorbing, miniaturist intricacy, *Marigolds in August* transcends this maze of practicalities. Ultimately, it is a film about manhood — and the impossibility of an African achieving manhood in a world which is geared to the white man's scheme.

Craig Raine, *Quarto*, London, No. 9 (Aug. 1980), p. 3

a: Novel

Tsotsi

Written: in 1959-61, then filed away; edited for publication only in 1980.
Published: Johannesburg: Quagga Press-Donker; London: Rex Collings, 1980; New York: Random House, 1980; London: Penguin, 1983; Johannesburg: Donker, 1989.

'Tsotsi' is the assumed name of a youthful Sophiatown hoodlum whose gang includes Boston, Die Aap, and the Butcher. Their lifestyle includes preying on rural gullibles, and the action opens with the murder of one of these. The demolition of Sophiatown occurs around them. By chance Tsotsi has a throw-away baby foisted on him and his attempts to nurture it disrupt the smooth workings of the gang — also triggering his own memories about his violent street-child origins. He dies diving into the rubble to rescue the baby as the bulldozers demolish his hideaway.

It is a strongly narrated and graphically credible novel. Future footnoters can have a field day recognizing here embryonic characters and incidents which appear again in Fugard's plays and filmscripts. It's astonishing that a writer known previously only for his dialogue should achieve such success with his descriptions of solitary action. I read *Tsotsi* expecting no more than a historically-curious annex to a major dramatist's career. I found instead an engrossing psychological thriller which is certainly one of the best novels in contemporary South African fiction.

Alastair Niven,
Times Literary Supplement, 2 May 1980

b: Autobiography

Notebooks (1960-77)

A selection of diary entries and notes on Fugard's life and work in the theatre, edited by Mary Benson.
Published: Johannesburg: Donker; London: Faber and Faber, 1983; New York: Knopf: 1984.

Notebooks (1960-77) *records Fugard's private struggle to become a public artist and to grasp the paradoxes of his troubled land. 'South Africa', he notes in 1963, 'needs to be loved now, when it is at its ugliest, more than at any other time'. Fugard expresses his own love by stubbornly remaining at home, and by using drama as a form of Gandhian non-violent resistance.*
Pico Iyer, *Time*, 30 Apr. 1984, p. 44

[On the key event in *'Master Harold' . . . and the Boys*.] Can't remember now what precipitated it, but one day there was a rare quarrel between Sam and myself. In a truculent silence we closed the café, Sam set off to New Brighton on foot, and I followed a few minutes later on my bike. I saw him walking ahead of me and, coming out of a spasm of acute loneliness, as I rode up behind him I called his name, he turned in mid-stride to look back, and, as I cycled past, I spat in his face. Don't suppose I will ever deal with the shame that overwhelmed me the second after I had done that.

Notebooks (1961), p. 26

The lies and half-truths that I have spread about Dad — alcoholic, fought in the war, etc. The truth — humility, resignation to suffering.

A character who deliberately propagates and establishes a public image compounded of cowardice, weakness, dependence of another man who was the exact opposite. But done, not out of hate, but in submission to the inevitability of his (the other man's — Dad's) fate — and, finally, love.

He was misunderstood: the silence taken for vacuity, the groans at night for weakness, the one leg for dependence.

Notebooks (1961), p. 31

I hesitate to put down this thought: that my death be so arranged that I can prepare. Now, thirty years old, feeling at times mortally sick from the corruption and duplicity of my country, I think that given time I could prepare, and find peace, by remembering, re-seeing, the little that I already have seen of life; and relive my dawning astonishment and wonder at the great beauty, complexity, and honesty of that vast area of 'living experiences' that have nothing to do with man.

Notebooks (1962), p. 48

[The 'pure theatre experience'] belongs to the audience. He is my major concern as a playwright. The ingredients of this experience . . . are the actor and the stage, the actor on the stage. Around him is space to be filled with movement; around him is also a silence to be filled with meaning, using words and sounds, and, at moments when all else fails him, including my words, the silence itself.

I write plays because I believe implicitly in the potential of this 'experience' as a means to approaching and transmitting the Truth, and in a way and with a force unique to drama. I believe equally strongly that this potential is at its greatest when the tricks associated with so much of present-day theatre are reduced to a minimum.

The cathartic possibility in theatre needs nothing more than the actor and the stage. For the miracle to happen it must come from within the actor. A good play will plant the seed there. Externals will profit the play nothing, if the actor has no soul.

'Introductory Note to *The Blood Knot*', *Contrast*, Cape Town, No. 5 (Autumn 1962), p. 29

So, *Johannesburg* again and another play under my arm [*People Are Living There*]. Vaguely ill-at-ease — discontented. The prospects ahead do not excite me as they would have in the past.

I look at the landscape out of the window and realize that South Africa's tragedy is the small, meagre portions of love in the hearts of the men who walk this beautiful land.

I fully expect a rather bewildered public reaction to this play if and when it reaches the stage. Bewildered because it might seem to be about nothing — and I know everyone is waiting for more controversy. I couldn't care less — the play concerns people and, most important of all, 'the noise of living'. The noise we must make, as Milly puts it, 'to let them know we are here'.

Notebooks (1963), p. 82-3

In the theatre of course my fascination lies with the 'living moment' — the actual, the real, the immediate, there before our eyes, even if it shares in the transient fate of all living moments. I suppose the theatre uses more of the actual substance of life than any other art. What comes near theatre in this respect except possibly the painter using old bus tickets, or the sculptor using junk iron and driftwood?

Which brings me to another fact about playwriting. As strongly, if not stronger, than the audience awareness of the actors and the living moment, there is the actor's awareness within that moment. Let me put it this way: there are two perspectives — from without, that of the audience; from within, that of the actor. My wholeness as a playwright is that I contain within myself both experiences — I watch and am watched — I examine the experience and I experience. The motion of a pendulum — or if that is too balanced and sane a movement — let me speak of agitation between two poles of awareness.

Notebooks (1963), p. 89

The Writer on His Work

The story of Dimetos in Camus's *Carnets*: falling in love with a beautiful but dead young woman washed up by the sea, and having to watch the decay and corruption of what he loves. Camus: 'This is the symbol of a condition we must try to define.'

When I first read his note on Dimetos I was excited and immediately thought of it as the germinal idea of a play. Yesterday I re-remembered it. Dimetos goes mad watching the decay of her body.

Notebooks (1963), p. 107

[The emergent theatre in South Africa] has involved co-operation, regardless of race, with mixed casts playing to non-racial audiences. This is the environment from which virtually all significant new play-writing emerges, and also represents the avant-garde in a stricter sense. It is this theatre, wrestling in local and universal terms with the agony and conscience of South Africa, that has eclipsed all other contributions in Africa.

I believe that the present situation in South Africa with its daily tally of injustice and brutality has forced a maturity of thinking and feeling, an awareness of basic values I do not find equalled anywhere in Africa.

In a sense this truly South African theatre is fighting a losing battle. There is a logic to oppression: it gets worse. We will never emerge into the twilight of respectability but, I fear, rather like moles, have to go underground in possibly all senses of the word.

'African Stages', *New York Times*, 20 Sept. 1964

Immorality Act case at De Aar. Coloured Anglican missionary and a forty-year-old white woman, a librarian. The police caught them in bed, pulled back the sheets and took photographs.

Darkness. Suddenly a blinding flash of light like a photographer's flash; a split second later a woman screams. Then stage lights up to reveal an office desk, chair, and — to one side — a filing cabinet. Standing at the desk, examining a police file, Sergeant.... He takes out a set of photographs — 'They'll get four months suspended.'

De Aar. Heat. Dust.

'Three statements after an arrest under the Immorality Act' — Woman Man Sergeant.

Notebooks (1966), p. 132-3

The point at which an image, or complex of images, ceases to be a 'personal fiction' and acquires a life of its own, a truth bigger than self. An unmistakable development, recognizable among other things for the new 'perspective' it gives to the 'self' that was living with them. A 'way' of seeing and responding to the world around me. Almost like a set of blinkers that focus my awareness on what relates directly to them, to the moments and incidents where they touch and correspond to the life around me.

Notebooks (1971), p. 194

I grew up in Port Elizabeth, in the back streets. And although our circumstances, though a bit crummy at times, weren't exactly squalid, that's where I got the feeling for the circumstances that provide the background to my plays.

Interview with Pat Williams,
Ink, 24 July 1971, p. 10

[An incident from 1972.] We climbed the thousands of feet to Buffelskop at the summit of the Cradock mountains, where Olive Schreiner, her baby, and her dog are buried. Guy Butler and I were joined by others including Athol Fugard the playwright, his wife Sheila, who is a novelist, and Don Maclennan, also a playwright. After a back-breaking climb we finally reached the top and flopped down exhausted. Athol, a wicked gleam in his eye, walked over to the stone sarcophagus, knocked on it and bent his ear to listen.

'Olive! Olive! Can you hear me? Richard's here to see you. Do you mind if he comes over?' He knocked again. 'Is it all right if Richard comes over?'

After listening a short while with his hand cocked over his ear he turned to me. 'It's all right; she's ready to receive you now.'

Richard Rive, *Writing Black*
(Cape Town: David Philip, 1981), p. 141

[On the various contributions made to the script of *Sizwe Bansi Is Dead*.] Because I am the eldest and the most professionally experienced I bring possibly an excess contribution to our work at the moment. I know something about what dramatic structure involves, and obviously I did a hell of a lot of the actual writing. But I've not been allowed inside a black township in South Africa for many years, so I am very dependent on John Kani and Winston Ntshona for a basic image, a vitality, an assertion of life.

Interview with Michael Coveney,
'Challenging the Silence', *Plays and Players*,
Nov. 1973, p. 35

I am a bastardized Afrikaner, a product of cultural miscegenation. I am a classic example of the guilt-ridden impotent white liberal of South Africa.

> Interview with Colin Smith,
> *The Observer*, 6 Jan. 1974

My plays have only two or three characters for several reasons. First of all, I write in the context of South African theatre, and the more economical my plays are the easier it is for them to get performances.

Secondly, my major influence is music, the most important composers to me being those who use one or two instruments — Bach, say, in his unaccompanied violin sonatas or cello suites. And so I think of actors as instruments. I've become an economical writer through circumstances and through personal predilection. I always strive for very tight plays. The tighter I can write them, the deeper I can get.

> Interview with Markland Taylor, *New Haven Register*,
> 13 Oct. 1974, p. 41

We've got to go on, hoping we'll get a second audience, knowing we live in a country with short horizons, with low-ceiling cloud. We've got to let ourselves go as far as we can, knowing that we are walking into a wall, or that our candles could be blown out by a wind we didn't anticipate.

This is one of the levels my play deals with. I hope I'm not becoming a propagandist in my old age. But I cannot deny this play has for one a real response for the specifics of this time and place — and the question of survival. It is called *A Lesson from Aloes*. A rather obvious lesson, perhaps. They survive the drought.

> Interview with Raeford Daniel, *Rand Daily Mail*,
> 25 Oct. 1978, p. 7

One of the things I had to do for a semester at Yale was to edit my notebooks for publication. I have to edit them because there's the question of finding a shape. In working through the material I was forced to consider the circumstances — how I managed, emerging from total orthodoxy, to end up, if you want to flatter me with a label, a dissident voice. I was subjected, just by the way the system works, to as much prejudice and inculcation of prejudice as other South Africans....

When I pass from being author to being director, I have to choose. But as author I could point to five or six directions that a specific moment could go with equal validity. As a director I can't play all of them. The one I choose reflects only my face as a director at that time. It isn't the definitive interpretation of the text.

Interview with Craig Raine,
Quarto, No. 9 (Aug. 1980), p. 11, 13.

The first thing I'd like to point out is that in the body of work that has my name, whatever its final value may be, I have used two radically different techniques — sets of tools, for that matter — in the making of a play. I like to use the word 'making' of a play to avoid any conceit about being an artist — that sounds very proud and affected. My profession is play-writing — a maker of plays, like the wheelwright and all the others.

The two radically opposed methods I have used are, first, the orthodox concept of a writer, which is somebody who disappears into his ivory tower with a stack of blank paper and emerges sometime later. It might take me a year to write a play; I'm very slow. The other technique I've used is to go into a rehearsal room — having given myself no time privately as a writer beforehand — with a loose mandate (an image, or sometimes more than that) and through work with actors, or using techniques like improvisation, I've evolved a text, an experience which we put on the stage. . . .

I've arrived at a stage where I really find myself almost incoherent when trying to explain the hows, whys, or whens of my operation as a playwright. And yet at the same time, I have a very secure sense of my own voice. My sense of myself is that I'm essentially a storyteller: I have on any number of occasions found myself saying and writing in my notebooks that the only safe place I've ever known is at the centre of a story as its teller.

Interview in *Momentum*,
ed. M. J. Daymond, J. U. Jacobs, and Margaret Lenta
(Pietermaritzburg: University of Natal Press, 1984), p. 22, 28

When I have insomnia, I have a mythical birthday party. The guests are all characters in plays I have written. Instead of counting sheep, I have to work out a seating arrangement to make sure I don't make the mistake of seating the wrong people together.

Interview with Paula Crouch,
The Atlanta Constitution, 1 June 1987, p. 7B

Home for me remains South Africa. I can still only write in South Africa. But I suppose I'm at a sort of high point in my career and that means that my earning potential in theatre overseas is very considerable, so I spend a lot of time there. . . .

Maybe here we have to look at our writers and see if they are living up to their responsibilities. The emergency clampdown may have had a stifling effect on writers here. It's a very disturbing thought. It's pretty scary — which, of course, is the whole object of the emergency exercise.

The most immediate responsibility of the artist here is to get people feeling again, to bring the experience immediately to the people. It is the moral responsibility of the artist in a repressive situation — in a situation where people are prevented at first hand from seeing what is happening. The moral responsibility of the artist is to keep alive a total awareness of the realities of our time.

Interview with Garalt MacLiam, Star, Johannesburg,
19 June 1989, p. 13

One of the reasons I've stayed viable as a writer is that I don't try to find out too much about myself, or why I do anything. If I want to do something, I do it. If I want to write something, I write it. I haven't lived my life according to a theory or a preconceived notion of where my art should go. I just operate from the guts.

Interview with Sean Taylor, City Late, Cape Town,
June-July 1989, p. 15

Like most South Africans, I have felt profoundly challenged by the dramatic developments of the past two months: challenged, among other things, to think about myself and my role as a writer in the free and open society everyone is talking about.

How would that role differ, if at all, from what it was in the brutally oppressive South Africa we are trying to break with? That thinking has involved something of a stocktaking of ideas, values, prejudices, and ideals I have as a political animal. And it involves a few questions. What do I need to keep? What should I get rid of? And, most important, what do I need that I haven't got?

A great deal has been said since that remarkable speech by State-President de Klerk on 2 February about the climate of trust needed to usher in the brave new South Africa. Trust is going to be the cornerstone of the future. It would be very short-sighted of us to think that external political devices evolved or dismantled at the negotiating table will by themselves be enough to ensure a just and decent society.

I have always believed that when the time came I would be able to make that trusting commitment without too much trouble or effort. I was wrong. To put it bluntly, I am going to have to do a lot of hard work on myself in order to come up with the degree of trust — with any degree of trust — asked for.

That stocktaking I referred to has been a very sobering experience. It has ended with me realizing that after forty years of trying to survive the pressures of an apartheid society, I have brainwashed myself into a set of hard and unyielding political attitudes. They are characterized by a deep scepticism and plain downright distrust of anything coming from the government. Distrust, deception, and just plain, no-frills dishonesty — those are now the real elements of the traditional way of life apparently kept very much alive by a government now asking for my trust.

In a recent television broadcast one cabinet minister said the time had come to forget the past. Full stop. That was it. The ease with which he said it left me speechless. It reflected a total insensitivity to and total lack of awareness of the damage done. The waste of human lives, during decades of National Party rule.

Instead of disarming me, it, in fact, feeds and deepens the distrust with which I now habitually examine anything coming from a government source. It strengthens my suspicion that the reform initiative does not represent the change of heart asked of me, but is rather a last-ditch political manoeuvre to stave off the loss of white privilege and political power.

There are most likely many other white South Africans who feel the way I do and almost certainly millions of black South Africans. This is a tragic state of affairs because unless the trust in the reform initiative is forthcoming, this society is heading for chaos. As is already obvious, the political temperature of South Africa is at boiling point. The onus is on the government to bring down the temperature. The only way to do so is to stop talking about dismantling apartheid and to do it. . . .

Address to the University of the Witwatersrand,
Johannesburg, *The Star*, 2 Apr. 1990, p. 13

a: Primary Sources

Bibliographic details of individual plays and published scripts for film and television will be found in Section 2, and of non-dramatic writing in Section 3.

Collections of Plays

Statements: Three Plays. London: Oxford University Press, 1974. [*Sizwe Bansi Is Dead*, *The Island*, and *Statements after an Arrest under the Immorality Act*.]

Dimetos and Two Early Plays. London: Oxford University Press, 1977. [*Dimetos*, *No-Good Friday*, and *Nongogo*.]

Selected Plays, ed. Dennis Walder. Oxford: Oxford University Press, 1987. [*Blood Knot*, *Hello and Goodbye*, *Boesman and Lena*, and *'Master Harold'... and the Boys*.]

My Children! My Africa and Selected Shorter Plays, ed. Stephen Gray. Johannesburg: Witwatersrand University Press, 1990. [*My Children! My Africa!*, *The Occupation*, *The Coat*, *Mille Miglia*, *Orestes*, and *The Drummer*.]

Articles and Essays

Most major articles by Fugard have been excerpted in previous sections, where bibliographic details will be found. See also his introductions, based on notebook entries, to Boesman and Lena and Other Plays, Statements, A Lesson from Aloes, *and* The Road to Mecca.

Interviews

Throughout his career Fugard has generously given interviews, particularly at the time of the premiere of one of his productions. The following list, arranged in chronological order by name of interviewer, is a selection of the more general and substantial pieces on his life and work, additional to those cited elsewhere in this volme.

Allister Sparks, *Rand Daily Mail*, Johannesburg, 24 July 1965, p. 8.

Robert Hodgins, *Newscheck*, Johannesburg, 21 July 1967, p. 24-9.

Don Maclennan, 'An Interview with Athol Fugard about *The Coat*', *The Coat* (Cape Town: Balkema, 1971), p. 1-6.
Naseem Khan, *Time Out*, 23 July 1971, p. 27.
Christopher Ford, *The Guardian*, 17 July 1971, p. 8.
Peter Wilhelm, 'Athol Fugard at Forty', *To the Point*, Johannesburg, 3 June 1972; reprinted in Stephen Gray, ed., *Athol Fugard*, p. 109-14.
Jonathan Marks, *Yale Theater*, IV, No. 1 (Aug. 1973), p. 64-72.
Garth Verdal, *Argus*, Cape Town, 13 Apr. 1974, p. 3-4.
Elenore Lester, *New York Times*, 1 Dec. 1974.
Melvyn Bragg, *The Listener*, 5 Dec. 1974, p. 734-5.
A. Christopher Tucker, *Transatlantic Review*, London, No. 53-4 (Feb. 1976), p. 87-90.
Roy Christie, *The Star*, Johannesburg, 7 Sept. 1976, p. 8-9.
Mary Benson, *Theatre Quarterly*, VII, No. 28 (1977), p. 77-83.
Barrie Hough, *Theoria*, Pietermaritzburg, LV (Oct. 1980); reprinted in Stephen Gray, ed., *Athol Fugard*, p. 121-9.
Mel Gussow, *The New Yorker*, 20 Dec. 1982, p. 47-94.
Garalt MacLiam, *The Star*, Johannesburg 18, 19, 20 Apr. 1983.
Ria Julian, *Drama*, London, No. 156 (Apr.-June 1985), p. 5-8.
Marilyn Achiron, *Interview*, New York, July 1986, p. 80-2.
Anne Sarzin, *Contrast*, Cape Town, XVI, No. 4 (Dec. 1987), p. 64-71.
William A. Henry, *Time*, 7 Aug. 1989, p. 56-8.
Rory Riordan, *Crux*, Pretoria, XXV, No. 1 (Feb. 1991), p. 3-14.

b: Secondary Sources

Full-Length Studies and Collections

Stephen Gray, ed., *Athol Fugard*. Johannesburg: McGraw-Hill, 1982. [Background pieces, reviews, interviews, and a selection of critical articles.]
Margarete Seidenspinner, *Exploring the Labyrinth: Athol Fugard's Approach to South African Drama*. Essen: Blaue Eule, 1986.
Russell Vandenbroucke, *Truths the Hand Can Touch: the Theatre of Athol Fugard*. New York: Theatre Communications Group, 1985; Johannesburg: Donker, 1986.
Dennis Walder, *Selected Plays of Fugard*. London: Longman; Beirut: York Press, 1980.
Dennis Walder, *Athol Fugard*. London: Macmillan, 1984 (Modern Dramatists Series).

Articles and Chapters in Books

Rob Amato, 'Fugard's Confessional Analysis: *'Master Harold'* . . . *and the Boys'*, in M. J. Daymond, J. U. Jacobs, and Margaret Lenta, eds., *Momentum: on Recent South African Writing* (Pietermaritzburg: University of Natal Press, 1984), p. 198-214.

Coleen Angove, 'Afrikaner Stereotypes and Mavericks in Selected Fugard Plays', *South African Theatre Journal*, Johannesburg, III, No. 1 (May 1989), p. 55-68.

Ronald Ayling, 'Literature of the Eastern Cape from Schreiner to Fugard', *Ariel*, Calgary, XVI, No. 2 (Apr. 1985), p. 77-98.

Mary Benson, 'A Hunger for Ideas Moves Them', *New York Times*, 12 Sept. 1965, p. 17.

Mary Benson, 'Athol Fugard and the Eastern Cape', in *A Far Cry* (London: Penguin, 1990), p. 186-215.

Robert L. Berner, 'Athol Fugard and the Theatre of Improvisation', *Books Abroad*, L (1976), p. 81-4.

J. M. Coetzee, 'Athol Fugard, *Notebooks (1960-77)*', *English in Africa*, Grahamstown, XII, No. 1 (May 1986), p. 96-100.

Derek Cohen, 'Athol Fugard's *Boesman and Lena*', *Journal of Commonwealth Literature*, XII, No. 3 (Apr. 1978), p. 78-83.

Derek Cohen, 'Drama and the Police State: Athol Fugard's South Africa', *Canadian Drama*, VI, No. 1 (Spring 1980), p. 151-61.

Derek Cohen, 'Beneath the Underworld: Athol Fugard's *Tsotsi*', *World Literature Written in English*, XXIII, No. 2 (Spring 1984), p. 273-84.

Jeanne Colleran, '*A Place with the Pigs*: Athol Fugard's Afrikaner Parable', *Modern Drama*, XXXIII, No. 1 (1990), p. 17-36.

Michael J. Collins, 'The Sabotage of Love: Athol Fugard's Recent Plays', *World Literature Today*, Summer 1983, p. 369-72.

Brian Crow, 'Empowering the People: African Theatre and Neo-Colonialism', *Australasian Drama Studies*, Brisbane, No. 15-16, (Oct. 1989-Apr. 1990), p. 71-83.

Errol Durbach, 'Paradise Lost in the Great Karoo: Athol Fugard's *Road to Mecca*', *Ariel*, XVIII, No. 4 (Oct. 1987), p. 3-20.

Errol Durbach, 'Surviving in Xanadu: Athol Fugard's *Lesson from Aloes*', *Ariel*, XX, No. 1 (Jan. 1989), p. 5-21.

Deborah D. Foster, '*The Blood Knot* and *The Island* as Anti-Tragedy', in Stephen Gray, ed., *Athol Fugard*, p. 202-17.

Patrick Gavigan, 'Playing out the Drama of Apartheid', *Third World Book Review*, London, II, No. 1-2 (1986), p. 85-91.

Stephen Gray, 'The Coming into Print of Athol Fugard's *Tsotsi*', *Journal of Commonwealth Literature*, XVI, No. 1 (Aug. 1981), p. 56-63.

A Select Bibliography

Stephen Gray, 'Athol Fugard's "Insubstantial Pageant": *The Road to Mecca*', *Australasian Drama Studies*, No. 7 (Oct. 1985), p. 45-52.

Michael Green, '"The Politics of Loving": Fugard and the Metropolis', *World Literature Written in English*, XXVII, No. 1 (1987), p. 5-17.

Robert Green, 'Politics and Literature in Africa: the Drama of Athol Fugard', in Christopher Heywood, ed., *Aspects of South African Literature* (London: Heinemann Educational, 1976), p. 163-73.

Robert Green, 'The Cripple and the Prostitute: Fugard's *Hello and Goodbye*', in Stephen Gray, ed., *Athol Fugard*, p. 163-75.

Jonathan Hammond, 'A South African Season: *Sizwe Bansi*, *The Island*, and *Statements*', *Plays and Players*, March 1974, p. 40-3.

Temple Hauptfleisch, 'Fugard's Dramatic Expression of the Freedom Concept in *Boesman and Lena*', in Stephen Gray, ed., *Athol Fugard*, p. 179-89.

Tamar Jacoby, 'No Place for Heroes', *New York Review of Books*, 19 Feb. 1981, p. 37-9.

Robert Kavanagh, 'After Soweto: People's Theatre and the Political Struggle in South Africa', *Theatre Quarterly*, VII, No. 33 (Spring 1979), p. 31-8.

Robert Kavanagh, 'Art and Revolution in South Africa: the Theatre of Athol Fugard', *African Communist*, London, No. 88 (1981), p. 40-53.

Robert Kavanagh, ' "No-Man's Land": Fugard and the Black Intellectuals', *Theatre and Cultural Struggle in South Africa* (London: Zed, 1985), p. 59-83.

Don Maclennan, 'The Palimpsest: Some Observations on Fugard's Plays', in Stephen Gray, ed., *Athol Fugard*, p. 217-23.

Margaret Munro, 'The Fertility of Despair: Fugard's Bitter Aloes', *Meanjin*, Melbourne, XXXX, No. 4 (Dec. 1981), p. 472-79. [Includes a record of Fugard productions in Australia.]

Margaret Munro, 'Research and Fugard', in Stephen Gray, ed., *Athol Fugard*, p. 143-51.

C. G. Okafor, 'Of Spooks and Virile Men: Patterns of Response to Imperialism in *Sizwe Bansi Is Dead* and *The Trial of Dedan Kimathi*', *Commonwealth*, Dijon, XII, No. 1 (Autumn 1989), p. 87-94.

Gerrit Olivier, 'Notes on Fugard's *"Master Harold"... and the Boys* at Yale Rep', *Standpunte*, Cape Town, No. 162 (Dec. 1982), p. 9-14.

Martin Orkin, 'Body and State in *Blood Knot/The Blood Knot*', *South African Theatre Journal*, II, No. 1 (May 1988), p. 17-34.

Patrick O'Sheel, 'Athol Fugard's "Poor Theatre" ', *Journal of Commonwealth Literature*, XII, No. 3 (Apr. 1978), p. 67-77.

Robert M. Post, 'Victims in the Writing of Athol Fugard', *Ariel*, XVI, No. 3 (July 1985), p. 3-17.

Robert M. Post, 'Racism in Athol Fugard's *'Master Harold' . . . and the Boys*', *World Literature Written in Emglish*, XXX, No. 1 (1990), p. 97-102.

Sheila Roberts, ' "No Lessons Learnt": Reading the Texts of Fugard's *A Lesson from Aloes* and *"Master Harold" . . . and The Boys*', *English in Africa*, XIX, No. 2 (Oct. 1982), p. 29-33.

Sheila Roberts, 'Fugard in the Seventies: Inner and Outer Geography', in Stephen Gray, ed., *Athol Fugard*, p. 224-32.

Anna Rutherford, 'Time, Space, and Identity in *The Blood Knot*', in Stephen Gray, ed., *Athol Fugard*, p. 151-62.

Brian Stone and Pat Scorer, 'Athol Fugard, *Sizwe Bansi Is Dead*', in *Sophocles to Fugard* (London: BBC, 1977).

Tom Stoppard, 'Fact, Fiction, and the Big Race', *The Observer*, 11 Aug. 1968, p. 20.

Russell Vandenbroucke, 'Robert Zwelinzima Is Alive', in Stephen Gray, ed., *Athol Fugard*, p. 190-7.

Gerald Weales, 'The Embodied Images of Athol Fugard', *Hollins Critic*, Virginia, XV, No. 1 (Feb. 1978), p. 1-12.

Richard Whitaker, 'Dimoetos to Dimetos: the Evolution of a Myth', *English Studies in Africa*, Johannesburg, XXIV, No. 1 (1981), p. 45-59.

Chris Wortham, 'A Sense of Place: Home and Homelessness in the Plays of Athol Fugard', in M. van Wyk Smith and D. Maclennan, eds., *Olive Schreiner and After: Essays on Southern African Literature* (Cape Town: David Philip, 1983), p. 165-83.

Reference Sources

Jeremy Fogg, 'Athol Fugard: Inventory of NELM's Holdings', Aug. 1989. [Items in the large collection of manuscripts, working scripts, drafts, production logs, translations, programmes, cuttings, correspondence, and personalia held by the National English Literary Museum, Private Bag 1019, Grahamstown, 6140, South Africa.]

John Read, *Athol Fugard: a Bibliography*. Grahamstown: NELM, 1991.

Temple Hauptfleisch, Wilma Viljoen, and Celeste van Greunen, *Athol Fugard: a Source Guide*. Johannesburg: Donker, 1982.

Russell Vandenbroucke, 'A Brief Chronology of Theatre in South Africa', *Theatre Quarterly*, VII, No. 28 (1977), p. 44-54.

Russell Vandenbroucke, *Athol Fugard: Bibliography, Biography, Playography*. London: TQ Publications, 1977 (Theatre Checklist No. 15).